Religion and the Decline of Capitalism

RELIGION AND THE DECLINE OF CAPITALISM

The Holland Lectures for 1949

by

V. A. DEMANT

CHARLES SCRIBNER'S SONS
NEW YORK

*First published in mcmlii
Printed in Great Britain by
Latimer Trend & Co Ltd Plymouth
All rights reserved*

The Holland Lectures

★

I. R. H. TAWNEY: *Religious Thought on Social Questions in the Sixteenth and Seventeenth Centuries* (March 1922). Published as *Religion and the Rise of Capitalism*.

II. CANON C. E. OSBORNE: *The Secular State in relation to Christian Ideals* (March 1925). Published as *Christian Ideas in Political History*.

III. WILLIAM TEMPLE (Bishop of Manchester): *Christianity and the State* (March 1928).

IV. A. D. LINDSAY (Master of Balliol): *Christianity and Economics* (March 1930).

V. SIR WALTER MOBERLY: *The Ethics of Punishment from a Christian Standpoint* (October 1933).

VI. DR. S. C. CARPENTER: *The Bible View of Life* (March 1936).

VII. DR. L. S. THORNTON: *Christ and Human Society* (October 1943 and March 1944).

VIII. M. B. RECKITT: *Maurice to Temple* (October 1946).

IX. DR. V. A. DEMANT: *Religion and the Decline of Capitalism* (October 1949).

Contents

★

Preface	*page* 11
I. The Great Reversal	13
II. Religious Reactions	35
III. Aims and Axioms	59
IV. The Political Faiths	86
V. The Criticism of Religion	109
VI. The Debate about Human Nature	134
VII. A Vicissitude of Civilization	157
VIII. God's Will and our Modern Age	177
Index	198

Preface

★

This piece of writing is an essay in the interpretation of our time. Its theme was developed in a course of the Scott Holland Memorial lectures first given at Oxford in the autumn of 1949. In the following year an abbreviated version of them was broadcast on the Third Programme in a series delivered before a public audience at Broadcasting House. In preparing them for publication as a book I have slightly enlarged upon some points in the lectures, but I have not thought it desirable to eliminate all expressions which indicate their original lecture form.

The subject was of course suggested by the first series of Holland Lectures given by Mr. R. H. Tawney in 1922, which was published in 1926 under the title of *Religion and the Rise of Capitalism*. Mr. Tawney was interpreting historic changes already three centuries old. My essay deals with the contemporary situation and its beginnings only a century back. Apart from its tentative character, which is the only appropriate one for an assessment of the significance of events in which we are still involved, my essay can claim no such command of historical material as that which marked Mr. Tawney's erudition. In my opening chapter I have tried to show the connection between the problems he handled and those with which I am concerned.

While the broadcast version of these lectures was in progress, Mr. George Bernard Shaw, shortly before his death, wrote to me saying that its title would lead to a confusion with the work of Sidney and Beatrice Webb, 'The Decay of Capitalism'. The Webbs' book was in fact called *The Decay of Capitalist Civilization*. Mr. Shaw's main point, however, was that both titles were mistaken, for, in his own words:

Preface

'Capitalism, far from decaying, has been carried to unprecedented magnitudes in the Tennessee Valley and elsewhere, and is culminating in state capitalism, *alias* communism, socialism, Fabianism, all requiring capitals beyond the means of private enterprise. Capitalism is an entirely uncontroversial term, like magnetism: civilization is impossible without it. There is no such alternative as capitalism versus socialism: the issue is between plutocracy and democracy. . . . This letter is for your consideration, not for argument, and needs no answer.'

I respected that last wish and sent no reply except to remind him of the correct title of the Webbs' work. But in the first and last chapters of this book I have sought to show my awareness of the point Mr. Shaw raised and, nevertheless, to justify the title I have used.

I record with immense gratitude my indebtedness to my colleague, Mr. M. B. Foster, Student of Christ Church, for his painstaking scrutiny of the proofs of this book. He has detected numerous errors, indicated many obscurities and challenged some statements. This has enabled me to correct the first, to remove (I trust) the second and to review the third with deference, in most cases though not in all, to his suggestions. The readers of a book never know how much they are spared by the one who risks a reputation by reading an author's proofs. In this case it is a great deal, and Mr. Foster should not be implicated in the faults which my ignorance, carelessness or obstinacy have caused to remain.

The tiresome task of typing at least two versions of these lectures has been generously carried out by Miss Diana Morshead, and I wish here to register my thanks to her. My son, Jocelyn, has given valuable help with the index.

V. A. DEMANT

Christ Church, Oxford
April 1952

CHAPTER I

The Great Reversal

★

It is twenty-seven years since the first series of Holland Memorial Lectures was delivered. A trust had been formed to commemorate the life and work of Henry Scott Holland, for twenty years Canon of St. Paul's, and for the last seven years of his life Regius Professor of Divinity in the University of Oxford. The commemoration was to take the form of a course of lectures to be delivered every three years having for their theme 'the religion of the Incarnation in its bearing on the social and economic life of man'. Holland was one of the few leading churchmen of his day who felt deeply that the rather subjective and pietist religion of England in his time was not ministering to the grave human and spiritual problems which beset men in the hey-day of the Industrial Age. The warrant for what he preached as the Christian witness in the social order he derived from his understanding of the Church's doctrine of the Incarnation. That this was Holland's central interest can be seen from some words of his, which must be judged from the standpoint, so far as we can recover it, of the middle eighties rather than from the more critical realism of the nineteen-fifties. 'From every side', he wrote, 'windows were flung open, barriers were thrown down, we were ready for a call and it came. From over the sea we began to be aware of a Social Philosophy which, however materialistic some of its tendencies might have become, has had alliance with the spiritual Hegelianism with which we had been touched. It took its scientific shape in the hands of Karl Marx, but it also floated across to us, in dreams and visions, using our own Christian language, and involving the unity of the Social

The Great Reversal

Body and the law of love, and the solidarity of Humanity. It read out the significance of citizenship in terms that were spiritual and Christian. It challenged us to say why we were not bringing our creed into action as the secret of all social well-being. Were we not engaged in asserting the pre-eminent value of the community over the individual by our faith in the Church? Were we not preaching the sanctity of human nature here on earth by our belief in the Sacraments? If we brought this creed to bear on Society, would it not show itself in the form of Christian socialism, as Maurice and Kingsley had understood it in the fifties? We woke up to Maurice. His influence, which had lain, as it were, alongside the Oxford Movement, now passed within it. . . . We had been shown by the Tractarians the depth and intensity of significance to be disclosed by faith in the Incarnation. Now we added to this a fuller estimate of the far-reaching extension of its meaning and the scope of its activities. Christian doctrine showed itself as the very heart of a Social Gospel.'[1]

We should use different language to-day, both for the theological and social concerns which Holland here expressed. My immediate predecessor in this lectureship, Mr. Maurice B. Reckitt, who has provided us with the fullest and brightest account of Anglican thought on social questions over the last hundred years, comments on this quotation: 'How faded now sounds that fifty-year-old phrase, yet how vital for us to-day the reality of which it speaks.[2]

Scott Holland seriously and concretely believed that the Incarnation, or God made man in a specific historic and social setting, was the decisive reason why, in his own words, 'Jesus Christ has a social and economic significance.' This could be guessed from the reminder that the quotation I have repeated at length comes from the introduction to addresses entitled '*Lombard Street in Lent*'.

When in 1922 Mr. R. H. Tawney inaugurated this lectureship with a work which has made history and provoked a string of reactions, to many people it was not obvious at first attention how an examination of the social changes in the sixteenth and neighbouring centuries could be regarded as a contribution to the theological theme set by the Scott Holland Trust. So much excitement was stirred up not only in the denominational world, but also in

The Great Reversal

that of the economists and historians, that the relevance of *Religion and the Rise of Capitalism* to a theology rooted in the Incarnation was treated as non-existent or artificial. Yet there were not wanting passages from the lectures themselves which disclosed how in the author's mind the two things were connected. The dissociation between religion and ethics on the one hand and social theory and practice on the other, which marks the transition to the modern world, is, he would contend, at variance with a true incarnational religion. Of the four possible attitudes to their relations Mr. Tawney assumed that the one predominantly characteristic of the Medieval World was that in which religious opinion 'accepts and criticizes, tolerates and amends, welcomes the gross world of human appetites, as the squalid scaffolding from amid which the life of the spirit must rise, and insists that this also is the material of the Kingdom of God'.[3] This attitude, he contended, was virtually eliminated by the religious and social changes of the fifteenth to seventeenth centuries, leaving the field for an unholy scramble between the other three, namely ascetic aloofness from a world given over to the Evil One; or indifference to a society with which religion has no concern; or agitation for a particular reform or revolution which its devotees identify with the realm of Grace. In particular the transference of economic life from having been a normative activity responsible to ethics and religion for its means and ends, to the achievement of autonomy, with a law of its own answerable to no other warrant—it is this transference in economic behaviour which, for our purpose in these lectures, is the significant fact which the first Holland lecturer did so much to illuminate.

Bishop Gore, in a preface to the original edition, wrote that 'the first series of Holland Lectures is a worthy tribute to the memory of a man who set his brilliant faculties to work in no cause so fully and heartily as in that of re-awakening the conscience of Englishmen to the social meaning of the religion of the Incarnation, and who felt as much as anyone the need of accurate research into the causes which have so disastrously obscured it'.

The intriguing question of how far the autonomy of secular disciplines in the last three centuries constitutes really a violation of a

The Great Reversal

Christianity which claims to be incarnational and sacramental is one we cannot embark upon, though at a later stage we shall have to see that some curious paradoxes arise in this matter. It might well have more attention given to it by dogmatic and moral theologians.

The publication of *Religion and the Rise of Capitalism* inaugurated an enlivened and enlivening debate; it engendered considerable heat which was often more obscuring than enlightening. Mr. Tawney has made his riposte to some of the adverse comment in his preface to the 1937 edition. The debate concentrated mainly upon the effect of the religious changes of early Protestantism on economic habits and theories; it was concerned especially with the views of Max Weber and others about the influences which had formed the climate in which modern commerce, industry and money-making could grow into social dominants. The debate became very much a Catholic-Protestant rivalry, with weapons varying with the position taken up as to whether capitalism was, like the monarchs of *1066 and All That*, a bad or a good thing. Those who thought it was bad, on both sides, spoke as one who should say: 'please, sir, it wasn't me'; or, 'I wasn't the only one'; or, 'the other boy led me on'. Those who thought it was good on balance, said as it were: 'why this scolding?' This thing capitalism is an essential step in the human enterprise; Christians should not resist the hand of God in world history but come to terms with it.' Some added: 'and religious forces reflected the social and economic changes rather than bringing them about'—an emphasis they would have found admitted and documented in Mr. Tawney's own work.[4] Others like R. S. Sleigh, a disciple of Ernst Troeltsch, valiantly took up the position that 'the insight of Calvin was not an illusion, for the relation between Christianity and capitalism is not accidental, but organic, intrinsically essential'.[5]

The debate, as it could be followed in English writings, has roughly three stages. In 1904 Max Weber had published his researches, part of which was later translated as *The Protestant Ethic and the Spirit of Capitalism*. Therein he deduced that capitalism with its *laissez-faire* doctrine and its conception of economic behaviour as autonomous, owing responsibility only to its own law,

The Great Reversal

along with its justification of business as 'a calling' or a religious vocation—that all this derived its warrant from Protestant and especially Puritan sources. Tawney's lectures to a large extent substantiated this thesis and also corrected it. Critics had pointed out that the spirit of capitalism was older than the Reformation. Tawney allows that it is as old as history. But he adds: 'it found in certain aspects of later Puritanism a tonic which braced its energies and fortified its already vigorous temper';[6] the main point being that it soon became regarded as a sign of religious seriousness instead of a menace to be suspected. In 1933 appeared a counterblast in Professor H. M. Robertson's *Aspects of the Rise of Economic Individualism: A Criticism of Max Weber and His School*.[7] He claimed that what he regarded as the Weber-Tawney thesis was more of a polemic weapon than a contribution to historic studies. Weber's essay on *Die Protestantische Ethik und der Geist des Kapitalismus* ushered in, says Robertson, as heavy an attack on the capitalist position as the materialist writings of Karl Marx. He adds: 'This is not immediately apparent; but even a cursory second glance shows that its general tendency is to undermine the basis of capitalist society.' In a more dispassionate vein, Robertson maintains that Weber failed to see that the notion of a 'calling', the sense of that station to which it shall please God to call us, when used by early Reformers, actually worked against acquisitiveness and in a conservative interest. True enough, but it does not dispose of Weber's question: How does 'the calling' come to have the commercial and acquisitive flavour it possessed by the eighteenth century? It was Tawney's main contribution to show how that came about.

Robertson produced plenty of evidence that at least one Catholic force made in the same direction, namely the casuistry which the Jesuits were elaborating to deal with the growing commercial and financial transactions of the time, especially in the matter of interest on money loans. This evidence was used to suggest that the Jesuit theology was too accommodating, that it exemplified the maxim 'there is nothing like business'—a charge already made in 1669 by Pirot and repeated by Groethuysen.[8] The Jesuit moralists, claimed Robertson, stripped their doctrine of those checks on gain which might seem hostile to the adolescent

The Great Reversal

bourgeoisie. An answer to this charge was made in 1934 by Father J. Brodrick in his book: *The Economic Morals of the Jesuits*.[9] The nearest thing we have to a summary of the debate is to be found in the work of Amintore Fanfani of Milan under the title: *Catholicism, Protestantism and Capitalism*, published 1935.[10] As a Catholic and a critic of capitalism he allows that capitalism arose in a Catholic world when the cupidity of some persons, making injustice for others, eventually resulted in the escape of business dealings from non-economic, that is, from ethical and social sanctions. It is true that the capitalist spirit, as defined most acutely in some ways by Werner Sombart, can be found in the ancient and medieval world; it is also true that the earlier Reformers were as uncapitalist in their outlook as their predecessors. But something was happening, and it might be epitomized by these sentences of Weber's: 'A state of mind such as that expressed in the passages we have quoted (from Franklin's *Necessary Hints and Advice to a Young Tradesman*) and which called forth the applause of a whole people, would both in ancient times and in the Middle Ages have been proscribed as the lowest sort of avarice and as an attitude entirely lacking in self-respect.'[11] He adds at a later point: 'Hence the difference does not lie in the degree of development of any impulse to make money,'[12] (as Sombart and Brentano assumed and, in consequence, pushed the origins of the capitalist spirit much further back[13]), but in the removal of 'an ethic based on religion which places certain psychological sanctions (not of an economic character) on the maintenance of the attitude prescribed by it, sanctions which, so long as the religious belief remains alive, are highly effective, and which mere worldly wisdom does not have at its disposal'.[14]

A sifting of the essentials of the controversy and a reading of the documents, in place of projecting upon writers what a critic feels sure the writer should be saying out of religious or social polemic attitudes, would, it seems, lead to a consensus of this kind:

What became economic individualism had been arrived at before the Reformation, but it was not acknowledged as moral, let alone regarded as a contribution to the general good. The early Reformers were as opposed to capitalist practices as the schoolmen

The Great Reversal

had been. The regions under Protestant influence capitulated first and co-operated in the transition in a way which has never been the case under catholic influence. And this is not just an idiosyncratic continental opinion. You can find the same judgement in economic historians, like Cunningham who wrote of seventeenth-century changes in government: 'The result was an immense development of economic freedom. . . . But this step was purchased at a heavy price. . . . Under these altered conditions no room was left for authoritative insistence on moral, as distinguished from legal, obligations; the success of Puritanism meant the triumph of the new commercial morality which held good among monied men; capitalists had established their right to secure a return for their money, and there was no authority to insist upon any corelative duty when they organized industrial undertakings and obtained control over the means of production.'[15]

It would perhaps not be profitable to recapitulate this debate any more fully, or to assess the correctness of explaining economic changes so largely by religious forces, or to apportion praise or blame on this side or that of the religious world. But the issue has to be recalled, if only in order to realize that all this literature is prompted by a very real question: what could possibly have brought about such a radical, unique and extraordinary change in human behaviour as that represented by the emergence of economic life as an autonomous activity? Their conclusions will not all stand, but if Tawney and the others had done nothing else but call attention to the revolutionary character of the transition and to the courage it required to break with tradition, they would have put into their debt all who desire to understand the turns of human history. In order to account for an entirely new relation of economic life to the rest of society they were compelled to seek for an influence so penetrating that they had perforce to look for it in religion, and thereby they started an inquiry which may throw some light upon the significance of changes in the nineteenth and twentieth centuries which, in cardinal though not in all respects, are in the reverse direction to those we have been glancing at.

The aim of these lectures is to pursue that inquiry into the contemporary situation. In order to estimate the force and meaning of

The Great Reversal

this great reversal, a reversal of all the tendencies which made for the independence of economic activity from the total demands of society and from ethics, it is necessary to look back a bit longer and consider what a highly specialized, unique and possibly irrepeatable phenomenon the achievement of economic autonomy really was. When we come to consider the changes of our own time, changes which make for the subordination of exchange, selling, production and money to other than economic requirements, it is well to do so with a clear understanding that what we are involved in is not a new mutation in the career of the human spirit, but in some sense a reversion to the kind of society which mankind has lived with for most of its enterprise on earth—a condition which has been broken into, and then not completely, by a highly interesting and significant interlude. The decline of capitalism is then to be regarded not so much as the beginning of a new order of history but as the end of a short-lived experiment. The business men and the economists who stood for the practice and theory of the free market in all things, in so far as it could be achieved—and who regarded it as of the essence of society—may not deserve, as we shall see they did not, all the abuse often levelled at them. But of one error they cannot be excused, though it is the most frequent error of the human mind when it is seeking to find a meaning to history. It is the error of regarding the relative positions reached at a certain time and often contingently beneficial at that time, as having an unchanging basis in Nature or in a pattern laid up in the heavens. Even so good a liberal as John Morley realized this: 'In a word they (the eighteenth-century philosophers) tried to understand society without the aid of history. Consequently they laid down the truths which they discovered as absolute and fixed, when they were no more than conditional and relative.'[16]

We have to see what it was which arose in this earlier period and is declining in our own time; then how unusual a development it was in the social history of man; further what is involved in the ending of its short life; and finally the significance for religion of this turn of events.

To give a scientific description of capitalism may be a hopeless task, but we can roughly identify as an historical phenomenon

The Great Reversal

something which Mr. Tawney has indicated by that term. Werner Sombart, in his article in the *Encyclopedia of the Social Sciences* (1937), draws out the confusing career of this word; it was first used widely with a controversial force only after the appearance of Karl Marx's *Das Kapital* and only in the twentieth century did it begin to be employed in academic economic discussion.[17] James Burnham, in his book, *The Managerial Revolution*, has given us as good an outline of its salient features as can be had in a small space.[18] For our purposes it is more to the point to observe that capitalism may be used, without bandying words, for one or all of three things: a form of economic organization, the mainspring of a certain kind of culture, and an outlook on the relation of the material universe to human existence. These aspects are intellectually separable; they have different historic spans and they are not coterminous. Consider, for example, some features of capitalist organization, like separation of owners and a labour force working for wages, and production for an expanding market. These and other traits could well be replaced by other forms of organization while such cultural results of capitalism as urbanization, subservience of life to economic purposes, technical incontinence, standardized recreations, bourgeois outlooks, continue to inform the succeeding collectivisms. Or if we look at the philosophy, we find that the assumptions of the 'Manchester School' about the natural law of economics, and self-interest directed by a hidden hand towards the general good, had roots in a period which preceded the appearance of large-scale manufacturing industry. It was only in this second phase that the term capitalism came into use also for the kind of society, as affected in its arts, education and daily habits, which was becoming merely the social clothing of the economic body. The three aspects must be distinguished, for their various rises and declines do not run together. When the economic organizations associated with capitalism are displaced, the cultural ends and means are often accepted without question by the following socialist régimes, and the 'naturalist' philosophies which grew up in the seventeenth and eighteenth centuries to underpin the economic age, may have a longer life still.

The feature of this phenomenon which is most germane to our

purpose in these lectures is the relative freedom of economic activity from social controls and its theoretical bulwark in the idea of economic life as the operation of natural law rather than a system developed by men. It might look as if this aspect of the economic organization of capitalism were of less concern to the theologian and moralist than the culture and philosophy which have been connected with its career. But, indeed, the assumption of the supposedly secular side of human existence is, or should be, of interest to the theologian even if the moralist stops short at a judgement of results. For one thing, the assumption that society was best served by all its constituent elements becoming subject to the market, where they become primarily the material of buying and selling, was in fact justified by an ethical proposition that there was a natural community of interests between the participators in the economic part of a society's life. This was the doctrine of Adam Smith, where we find it at its most judicious, and of Mandeville, whose *Fable of the Bees* puts it at its most provocative. Besides the ethics there was also a cosmology or philosophy in the minds of the upholders of the free market or *laissez-faire*. It was the doctrine of the hidden hand which, behind the scenes of human will and intelligence, made all things work together for good whether men loved God or not. These axioms seem to us to-day so odd, that we shall later have to ask how men could mistake for Nature and account for by an absurd moral calculus, what now appear to be the temporary benefits of very contingent circumstances. What we are trying to get at now, however, is not the theory behind the economy of a 'free-market-in-all-things', but the extent to which both the practice and the theory belong to a peculiar combination of historical circumstances (economic, political, philosophic and religious) which, looked at with the eyes of an historian of human cultures, must be regarded as a sociological abnormality.

I am aware that I am making a controversial assumption in suggesting that the nerve of capitalism is the predominance of market relationships over the greater part of the social field. But it does underlie most if not all the characteristics which both defenders and attackers of capitalism have recognized as belonging to it, such as for example concentrated property in the instruments of

The Great Reversal

production, labour as a commodity whose price is regulated by its sale in the market, or the pervasive use of money in exchanging the products of the division of labour. If we may state the main problem set by the capitalist phase of history as the achievement of great economic advantages at the cost of colossal social dislocations, then our assumption that capitalism in its total aspect means the running of a society as an adjunct of the market relationship, helps us to see where the main dislocations lie. A powerful case can undoubtedly be made out for separating the free market economy from other factors which are alleged to have produced the dislocations, such as the argument recently advanced by Professor Röpke of Geneva.[19] But I have yet to find an answer to the case advanced by Karl Polanyi in his study of the Industrial Revolution.[20] This case draws on history to show that the process by which more and more factors in human life become marketable, that is to say, subject to price, demand, supply, and exchange, reaches its climax of social destructiveness when the three foundations of society, which are not by their nature commodities, are treated as if they were, namely labour, land and money. Professor Clapham has suggested that the factory system called for this development.[21] Because technical equipment is expensive, large amounts of material must be acquired and goods sold. When the machine appears, cost is a function of quantity. Therefore all the factors involved must be available in the necessary quantities to any who can pay for them. There must be no discouraging placards 'not for sale' set up in the interests of the non-economic concerns of living—of the concerns of kinship, of neighbourhood, of profession or creed. Everything must be open to freedom of contract. Incomes must only be formed through sales of labour or financial accommodation and prices must be formed by the self-regulation of the market. The organic bonds grown by society were to be loosened or snapped and all non-contractual relations discouraged.

There is now a large literature from the pens of anthropologists and social historians to show that the domination of social relationships by the economic functions is a unique phenomenon of the last few centuries; never before our own modern times did sale and exchange in the commercial sense constitute more than the

The Great Reversal

fringes of economic life. When all economic relations tend to become market transactions, then the very substance of social living is endangered. It is only because society by its toughness was not completely amenable to market economy that capitalism was possible even for a short time and has some great achievements in the productive field to its credit. A self-regulating market society has never existed in its entirety; it could be approached and could achieve solid results only so far as there were underneath it non-contractual organic bonds (legal, moral and religious). Pirenne and other economic historians have shown that commercial transactions as the predominant form of economic mutuality within localities were a late development compared with external trade.[22]

It can be said that industrial capitalism as a social system did not arrive until the competitive labour market was finally established in 1834.[23] A recent writer on the History of Economics suggests that 'the time which saw the origin of the marginal utility doctrine, the years 1854-74, mark the climax of capitalist development'.[24]

The uniqueness of the phase we are considering, its unnaturalness, as it were, needs perhaps little further emphasis, though the fact that this unnaturalness contradicts the whole intellectual apologia for the system is perhaps not made enough of in interpreting the ways of the human mind in justifying certain types of behaviour. Let us look at the uniqueness a little further: 'The isolation of economic aims as a specialized object of concentrated and systematic effort', wrote Mr. Tawney, 'the erection of economic criteria with an independent and authoritative standard of social expediency, are phenomena which, though familiar enough in classical antiquity, appear, at least on a grand scale, only at a comparatively recent date in the history of later civilizations,'[25] and he concludes: 'unless industry is to be paralysed by recurrent revolts on the part of outraged human nature, it must satisfy criteria which are not purely economic.'[26]

We can get an inkling as to how the earlier classical economists could be brought to regard the free market as the natural state of man, if we appreciate that in a sense the science itself can only handle those phenomena which approach a state of freedom in

The Great Reversal

exchange and sale. Walter Bagehot realized this, with approbation of the new turn in what he regarded as social evolution. In *Physics and Politics* he wrote: there had once been 'a sort of pre-economic age when the very assumptions of political economy did not exist, when its precepts would have been ruinous and when the very contrary precepts were requisite and wise'.[27] Dr. Löwe holds that: 'there are some exact laws of exchange. They are calculable in objective magnitudes, but they are valid only for one special order of the market, based on a particular constellation of sociological elements.'[28] In other words, the calculability of market relations is not to be attributed to the pure essence of economic behaviour but to some sociological condition which approaches a pure market relationship. 'In Adam Smith's time the estates of feudalism were already dissolved, the classes of capitalism not yet formed . . . never was society nearer to the ideal of perfect equality,'[29] and in consequence the socialist F. Lassalle thought that 'in an equalitarian social order the free operation of self-interest could in fact be to the common advantage'.[30]

Two other generalizations need recording before we can assess the significance in this century of the disappearance of the free market as dominating society, and consider its religious implications.

One is the fact that a century of almost unbroken peace, from 1815 to 1914, when the market economy did achieve its greatest economic triumphs, encouraged the notion that an increase of contractual relationships made for the diminution of conflict. Cobden, Bright, Herbert Spencer, J. S. Mill, Proudhon and even the *Communist Manifesto* made this assumption. The notion had a long hangover. As a hardened reviewer of books on the great Depression in the 1930's, I remember the refrain running through most of them: 'economics are good for peace, politics are bad.' This was perhaps plausible during a certain period of the last century 'when domestic capitalism on the basis of the division of labour among the economically developed and the backward countries seemed to have room for ever expanding foreign trade'.[31] That is to say, the alleged 'eternal' laws of classical economics, which assumed free trade and free competition, were valid only under certain social and political conditions.

The Great Reversal

The other generalization of importance for our problem is that this uniqueness of the capitalist phase in history is an accompaniment of, and looks as if it belonged inseparably to, a larger setting of social development.

On one hand this phase has historically gone with the enormous strides taken in technique and science. 'Only in the last four hundred years', writes Karl Jaspers, 'has a radical difference between Europe and China and India appeared, namely that of universal science and technique.'[32] Max Weber made it his special interest to ask what is peculiar to the West. Why did capitalism arise here? and one might add, why is its culture now spreading to the East and Africa even though it goes under socialist rather than capitalist aegis? On the other hand, too, this development of economic rationality, as Sombart calls the spirit of capitalism, has some historic connection with the whole development of the liberal society in its positive aspects. These aspects were represented by the pursuit of truth independent of social convenience, by moral criteria which are more ultimate than labels of a particular sect struggling for survival or supremacy in the scramble of life, by a universal justice available for all men by recognition of a certain equality in the depth of man's being which cannot be recognized so long as he is seen as nothing but a functional part of a closed organic grouping. All that characterized civilization as transcending merely tribal culture—all this with its roots in Greek rationality, in Roman trans-local politics and in Judaeo-Christian religion—all this is in some way the Western achievement *par excellence*, and it is out of this development that the market economy with its abstraction of one element in human society has sprung. This poses part of our problem. Can economic liberalism go down without losing firstly the advantages of disinterested science and serviceable techniques, and secondly such positive aspects of the liberal tradition as the rule of law and insistence upon the priority of persons over institutions? There are powerful voices on both sides of the argument. Some proclaim that in spite of the social dislocations of the last two centuries a free market economy is inseparable from the liberal and democratic values. Others aver that the disintegration of society by the hypertrophy of the market economy is so radical that only

The Great Reversal

by a rigid subordination of the market to social controls for non-economic ends will liberty be preserved or recovered. Others, again, that the exigencies of economic justice and social cohesion are so overriding that the liberties which have gone with the free market and are inseparable from it, may well have to be sacrificed. We shall consider these matters; in particular the questions posed by the collapse of the liberal experiment in economic life which is known as capitalism, and by the danger of losing the elements of the classical, Christian and liberal culture of the West along with it.

This twentieth century of ours is witnessing on a widespread scale the disappearance of the economic autonomy of the capitalist era. The beginning of this reversal goes a good deal further back.[33]

We may say in fact that it began even before the high-water mark of market economy was reached. Like a famous advertisement, we can say 'That's Capitalism, that was'.

Society soon began to protect itself from the ravages of purely competitive relations. As early as 1795 the Speenham land law for a minimum income irrespective of wages prevented labour for a time from being treated as a vendible commodity left to find its place in the market.

In the nineteenth century more and more movements arose to intervene and interfere with the free play of the market economy. Poor relief and other *ad hoc* measures were part of this trend. Much more deliberate were the growth of socialist movements and self-subsistence theories such as those connected with Robert Owen in this country, with the French socialists and then with Marxist communism. The force of these reactions resided and still resides in at least three features: in their response to claims of economic justice which was known to be violated by the inhumanities of a *laissez-faire* economy; in the extent to which they gave the artisan section of society a promise of economic improvement; and, what is perhaps more significant, in a doctrine, especialy in Marxism, which offered men an explanation of what was happening. This opportunity of mental mastery over their fate, compensating as it did for the loss of responsibility and sense of significance in work, even without great practical results, has been a profound influence in the growth of socialism. As in many other cases in history the opponent was not weakened by the attack, it was attacked because it was weakened. The explanations offered for the weakening of the capitalist order, such as its internal crises and diminishing loyalty to it, the failure of its promises to bring about a steady and irreversible march towards universal prosperity, peace and democracy—the rationale which socialist theories offered of all this must be accounted as one of their greatest assets in winning support.

But capitalism has had its critics and opponents who are not upholders of socialist theories and collectivist politics, and as Professor Carr has shown, changes in the international field have steadily deprived the economies of the older industrialist societies of their essential modes of activity.[34] In the work of Peter Drucker is to be found a non-socialist diagnosis of what he calls 'The End of Economic Man'.[35] An American expert in industrial organization holds that 'Modern industrial society suffers from a dangerous lack of social integration, and certain characteristics of industrial activity are likely to increase this condition unless steps be taken to prevent it'.[36] The main task of statesmanship to-day is to find what those steps are to be. Where planning now mostly takes the form of collectivizing an atomistic society already *disorganized* in the literal meaning of the word, a real leadership commensurate with the scale and depth of the problem would envisage the formidable task of re-creating a more natural community so well grounded in its biological, community and spiritual foundations, that it can use technique and exchange as enrichments without drying up the sources of social living.

The late Professor Elton Mayo who had studied the effect upon social loyalties of the American factory system had remarkable results in giving advice to management as to how to foster co-operative attitudes therein. Having put himself to school with sociologists like Le Play, Durkheim and Christopher Dawson, he has shown how rapid industrial and technical development, quite apart from economic rewards and penalties, has undermined spontaneous social co-operation such as is universal in pre-capitalist societies.[37] He reaches two conclusions of some importance. One, that both the hypothesis of a rabble of unrelated individuals (which

The Great Reversal

underlies the free-market theories) and the conception of an all-powerful state, which arises to re-order the rabble, have the same roots—namely weakening of all the natural associative forms of human grouping, the family, the church, the club, the guild and the university. His second conclusion is that there are two principles of social organization: that of established society and that of an adaptive society. Established societies are those which obtain everywhere before the capitalist era, represented by the primitive tribe, the early industries of New England and the small Australian cities of 1880. He points out that most revolutionary movements are impelled by a desire, largely unconscious, to return from present uncertainty to established certainty. They are in fact reactionary and the wiser for that. Adaptive society is the one made necessary by the transcending of local economies, by specialization in production and large-scale industrial and urban centres. Mayo hopes for an increase in human adaptiveness, for the alternative is, he would claim, a loss of the benefits of modern technique.

I mention this interesting contribution to our subject without accepting the latter conclusion. I think a different conclusion must be drawn. Mayo's studies suggest that men can be adaptive in some activities in a society which is established in respect of other and more fundamental activities. But he counts too much upon an unlimited power of adaptation to any change of social structure which diminishes its established elements. In fact one of the salient factors which accounts for the decline of the free-market economy is that it presumed upon a degree of adaptability which it is beyond the powers of the human being to achieve. For, only when men are settled in some of their relationships are they free to act and be adaptive in others. The economic freedom of capitalism was possible so long as it did not occupy the whole field. And the market economy as a formative influence on society is now in decline because its achievements depended upon its resting on top of a solid layer of non-economic relationships which it proceeded to obliterate. A defender of the market economy, Professor Röpke, has recognized this: 'It was', he says, 'the cardinal fault of the old liberal capitalist thought to regard the market economy as a *self*-dependent process whirring away automatically. It was overlooked that the market represents but one narrow sphere of life, a sphere which is surrounded and kept going by a more comprehensive one; a wider field in which mankind are not merely competitors, producers, men of business, members of unions, shareholders, savers and investors, but are simply human beings—men as members of their family, as neighbours, as members of their church, as colleagues, as citizens of the community, men as creatures of life and blood with their sentiments, passions and ideals. That is to say market economy requires a firm framework which, to be brief, we will call the anthropo-sociological. If the frame were to break, then the market economy would cease to be possible.' Röpke adds: 'It is just because of the rotten condition of this supporting framework that the liberal economic structure of the past, together with its social system, has fallen down.'[38] He does not admit the possibility, which I believe must be recognized, that the very extension of market economy, with the mechanization of the industrial revolution, the high degree of specialization between economic areas and between land and city—that these things have impaired and eaten into the organic foundations of society and could not do otherwise.

We shall have to return to consider other aspects of this phase of the decline of capitalism, aspects which relate the decline to the destruction of the non-economic levels on which it depended—a process continued by its socialist successors. Here it is only necessary to refer to some studies which establish a kind of law of diminishing returns—to put it at the mildest—in the development of the market economy of industrial civilization. Much has been said by Joseph A. Schumpeter on the way in which the success of capitalism has broken up its own institutional framework as well as the layer of feudal relationships which underlay it.[39]

Furthermore, to relate the problem to the converse one raised by Mr. Tawney in his first Holland Lectures, it seems that the career of capitalism has destroyed and is destroying the dispositions which engendered it. The bourgeois dispositions which the capitalist epoch developed were not the same as those which inaugurated the capitalist enterprise. The sense of being 'called' to serve God and earn one's eternal destiny by prowess in the world's

The Great Reversal

affairs; the ascetic and self-denying habits which made this possible; the energy and courage which staked a chance on new business undertakings—all those virtues or vices which Weber and Tawney have identified as the psychological springs of capitalism—represent, however perverted and uprooted from their seedbeds, dispositions carried over from the cultures in which the religious, heroic, chivalric, adventuring, ascetic and self-denying virtues were reared. The bourgeois attitude which capitalism has fostered in their place is rationalist, bargaining and unheroic. It has completely killed the sense of vocation. It has evaporated the elementary communal loyalties of the natural man and presented him with the dreary alternative of either looking after number one only or devotion to an abstract good of the community as a whole, which alleged good he cannot see has anything to do with the needs of his family and fellow beings in the concrete. 'The stock exchange is a poor substitute for the Holy Grail,' writes Schumpeter, for there was a psychic disposition in the origin of capitalism akin to the quest of the Holy Grail, which the success of bourgeois culture has entirely displaced.

I have suggested four main reasons for the decline of capitalism: the hostility it has brought on against itself; the break-up of its own institutional framework; its parasitism on the non-economic foundations of society; and the dissipation of the dispositions which reared and sustained it.

Whether this diagnosis is correct and complete or not, the fact is undeniable that in countless ways—by attack, by *ad hoc* measures, by drift—the process of emancipating the economic functions from the biological, moral, and community demands of society is being reversed. Producing, exchange, professional service—are less and less determined in their magnitude and direction by the price they can command on the free market, and more and more upon non-economic requirements, demands or dictatorial orders.

Here emerges the serious problem and many subsidiary ones to which we shall give attention, for it raises questions which no religious believer or moralist or legislator or teacher, can quite ignore. While society itself is bringing economic life into tutelage again, what the twentieth century is tending towards is not what the sixteenth departed from. The question then arises: are the collectivisms of our secularized age in any sense due to the pull of perennial needs of man which were ministered to, with all their crudity and sinfulness, by the more organic societies which the rise of capitalism tended to disintegrate?

The questions crop up thick and fast: was the ethically normative character of economic life in the Middle Ages something which can be counted on to return just because the free-market economy which was associated with its disappearance is itself becoming a thing of the past? Let us pose a deeper question still. The independence which economic activities gained was brought about within the bounds and ethos of Christendom, and has some derivative links with the classical Christian tradition. And the embedding of economic processes in non-economic social relations is not peculiar to early or medieval Christendom; it is a feature of the ancient Mediterranean world, of the pagan empires of antiquity and of the tribal life of Oriental and primitive peoples. We may then ask: in what sense is humanity's struggle to recover from the dissociation represented by the rise of capitalism, a reversion to a state of life which classical and Christian culture transcended?

When reactions against the free market and its human results are seen to be tied up with movements which appear to overturn not only the economics of the liberal age but the whole Western tradition with its fostering of legality, of science, of the division of powers—can we envisage any other result of the submergence of economic life in the social structure again, than a reversal of the whole civilized enterprise? What estimate of human nature are we counting on; is it too good or too bad for capitalism? How can hope be rekindled when the secular faith in progress is waning? What is Christendom, or its remnants, to say to the masses outside it in Asia and Africa who are now in revolt against the economic forces capitalist society has brought to bear on them, while at the same time they are moved by envy and misguided emulation of many of its destructive cultural features?

If the capitalist phase of human history has in it a self-defeating mechanism, or to vary the metaphor, if it kicks away the ladder up which it has climbed, is this a universal characteristic of all advanced social structures, and can any of its successors escape the same fate? These and many other questions arise and cannot but bring perplexities to the religious consciousness.

NOTES

1. H. Scott Holland, *Lombard Street in Lent* (Introduction to new edition 1911).
2. M. B. Reckitt, *From Maurice to Temple* (Scott Holland Memorial Lectures, 1946), pp. 120-1.
3. *Religion and the Rise of Capitalism* (1927), p. 17. (Pelican ed. 1938, p. 33.)
4. Especially op. cit. n. 32, p. 319. (Pelican ed., p. 283) and Foreword to Max Weber, *The Protestant Ethic* (Eng. tr., 1930).
5. R. S. Sleigh, *The Sufficiency of Christianity* (London, 1923), p. 160.
6. Tawney, op. cit. p. 226 f. (Pelican ed., p. 204.)
7. (Cambridge, 1933.)
8. *Origines de l'Esprit Bourgeois en France*, 2nd ed. (Paris, 1927).
9. (Oxford, 1934.)
10. Eng. tr. London, 1935, with a very full Bibliography.
11. *The Protestant Ethic and the Spirit of Capitalism* (Eng. tr. 1930), p. 56.
12. Ibid., p. 57.
13. Werner Sombart, *Der Moderne Kapitalismus* (Munich, Leipzig, 1902-24); L. Brentano, *Die Anfänge des Modernen Kapitalismus* (Leipzig, 1923).
14. Weber, op. cit., p. 197, n. 12. For full list of Weber's work, *vide*: *Bibliography on Max Weber*, by H. Gerth and Hedwig Gerth in *Social Research* (New York), vol. XVI, March 1949.
15. W. Cunningham, *The Growth of English Industry and Commerce in Modern Times* (Cambridge 1903), vol. I, p. 206.
16. *Critical Miscellanies* (London 1886), vol. II, p. 219.
17. *Encyclopedia of the Social Sciences* (1937): 'The term Capital has been used in English since the early seventeenth century to convey the meaning of accumulated wealth underlying industrial activities.' For further discussion of the origin of the term Capitalism, cf. articles in *Encyclopedia Britannica*.
Adam Smith, in much of Book II of *The Wealth of Nations*, described the function and operation of capital, but had only one use of the word 'capitalist', not 'capitalism' at all. The term crept in during the early nineteenth century, largely through the influence of the *Communist Manifesto*, where this statement occurs: 'In Bourgeois Society, capital is independent while the living person is dependent and has no individuality.' The earliest use of the term known to a modern student is in 1588, cf. R. D. Richards, 'Early History of the Term Capital', *A Quarterly Journal of Economics*, vol. XI, February 1926.
18. *The Managerial Revolution* (Pelican Books), p. 13 ff.
19. Wilhelm Röpke, *Civitas Humana*, Eng. tr. 1948.

The Great Reversal

20. Karl Polyani, *The Origins of Our Time* (1944): 'A market economy is an economic system controlled, regulated and directed by market prices; order in the production and distribution of goods is entrusted to this self-regulating mechanism. An economy of this kind derives from the expectation that human beings behave in such a way as to achieve maximum money gains.'—p. 74.
21. J. H. Clapham, *Economic History of Modern Britain*, vol. III.
22. H. Pirenne, *Economic and Social History of Medieval Europe*, p. 142.
23. K. Polanyi, op. cit., p. 88.
24. W. Stark, *The History of Economics*, 1944, p. 55, n. 2.
25. Tawney, op. cit., p. 278 (Pelican ed., p. 246).
26. Ibid., p. 284 (Pelican ed., p. 251). cf. R. M. MacIver, 'Never before the industrial age was economic power really separable from the political.'—*The Modern State* (1926), p. 138.
27. New Edition, pp. 11 and 12.
28. Adolf Löwe, *Economics and Sociology*, 1935, p. 72 ff.
29. Stark, op. cit., p. 25.
30. F. Lassalle, *Arbeiterprogram*, ed. 1874, pp. 31 ff.
31. H. J. Morgenthau, *Scientific Man versus Power Politics*, 1947, p. 77.
32. Karl Jaspers, *The European Spirit*, 1948, p. 32.
33. cf. E. Lipson, *The Growth of English Society*, 1949, especially chap. X.
34. E. H. Carr, *Conditions of Peace*, 1942.
35. Peter Drucker, *The End of Economic Man*, 1939; and *The Future of Industrial Man*, 1943.
36. T. N. Whitehead, *Leadership in a Free Society* (Harvard), 1936.
37. Elton Mayo, *The Social Problems of an Industrial Civilization* (Harvard), 1945.
38. op. cit., pp. 31, 32.
39. Joseph A. Schumpeter, *Capitalism, Socialism and Democracy*, 1943, pt. II.

CHAPTER II

Religious Reactions

★

The period of capitalist economic enterprise cannot be precisely dated. Throughout its career it has existed side by side with two other forces: non-economic social structures and forms of behaviour which have limited the free pursuit of economic advantage, and secondly, a number of economic relations not completely determined by the free play of market interactions. 'Not until the 1830's did economic liberalism', says a recent writer, 'burst forth as a crusading passion, and *laissez-faire* become a militant creed.'[1] It took from the sixteenth to the nineteenth century for the new conception of autonomy—in this matter autonomy of the economic function in society—to become embodied as the formative factor in the workings of modern industrial society.

This conception of autonomy or independence of economic forces and motives had first arisen in connection with trade and commerce and only later was it engaged with instruments of production, and last of all with buying and selling in such basic factors as land, labour and the means of exchange. The emancipation of the economic function and its climax in the theory and practice of making all relations subservient to the free play of market values—this emancipation had considerable religious implications. Not only had economic conduct before the change been regarded as a branch of ethics—this was acknowledged even when disobeyed—also, whatever there had been of economic regulation and theory had been a normative discipline like the rest of legislation. The transition from that state of affairs to the modern period meant that this field of human life had no longer to receive its warrant from ethical, legal, local or non-economic requirements, let alone supernatural ones. This itself posed a problem to religious thought. We know it was but one element in a larger process by which many of society's functions, like law, education and science, were acquiring their independence of an overarching philosophy which was closely geared to Christian theology.

This independence in the economic sphere was not, as a fact, carried out under the impulse of a move towards atheism. On the contrary, its sponsors elaborated a theology of their own and a moral calculus, to justify this momentous historical transition. Those early modern economists called the Physiocrats, who had not gone so far from original social righteousness as their successors of the classical school, proclaimed a religious philosophy which virtually equated '*Physiocratie* with *Theocratie*'. It amounted to this in the words of Mercier de la Rivière: 'The great order of nature which they proposed to investigate was to them the law which Providence, the Highest Being, the Author of Nature, the Founder and Legislator of human society, had given to the universe. All our interest, all our wills tend to unite and to form for our common happiness a harmony which we can regard as the work of a beneficent deity who wills that the earth should be covered with happy men.' F. Bastiat declared: 'The social mechanism . . . reveals the wisdom of God and proclaims His glory.' (*Harmonies Economiques*, 2nd ed., 1851.) This theology of 'the pre-established harmony' with which the Creator makes all men's uncontrolled economic impulses minister to the good life, was dominant in the earlier commercial period from 1750–60 and then between 1820–30 when industrialism was near reaching its climax in a flood of productive success and social dislocation.[2]

With regard to this new religious doctrine of the natural world as the providential link between the Creator and human society— God, the world, and society, being three aspects of the unity of existence—it is of interest to note that half-way through the nineteenth century John Stuart Mill came to doubt its validity for one part of the economic process: 'The laws and conditions of the production of wealth partake of the character of physical truths . . . it

Religious Reactions

is not so with the distribution of wealth. That is a matter of human institution solely. . . . The distribution of wealth depends on the laws and customs of society.'[3] Only the productive part of economic activity is an operation of physical laws. Mill is half-way to the communist Bukharin, who wrote: 'In a socialist society, political economy will lose its *raison d'être* . . . for . . . the causal consequences in the life of the unbridled element will be replaced by the causal consequences of the conscious performances of society.'[4]

This, however, has carried us for a moment beyond the immediate point that the system variously called Manchester Economics, *laissez-faire* or free-market economy, was held to be the system which Nature herself had dictated. This brings the question into close contact with those theological traditions which are concerned in an entirely different sense with the *Lex Naturae*. Before we approach that aspect of our problem there are some other reasons to be listed for seeing how the rise of capitalism and its setting were bound to provoke certain religious reactions. First of all there was a theological reason. Capitalism was part of the whole movement known as liberalism by which the harmony of interests was presumed as a metaphysical fact and something to be recovered by human nature in its struggle to overcome the dissociative forces of egoism, pride and power striving. It was this liberalism which dispensed with 'the sacred' as a real element in existence and gave the 'secular' all the religious valuations previously accorded to the divine realm; which slurred over the contradiction in the centre of man's nature, the tragedy of evil, thinking to overcome it by the freedom of reason; it was this liberalism which Newman attacked as something in the struggle convulsing European society, which brought out the age-long warfare of the Two Cities, the earthly and the heavenly—or as R. W. Church put it: 'the tendencies of modern thought to destroy the basis of revealed religion and ultimately of all that can be called religion at all.'[5]

Secondly, there were pastoral reasons. The Christian Church had an anxiety over the process by which society ceased to be a *communitas communitatum*, its members linked by natural and historic ties. The supervening bonds of contract only, which tended to make men related only as economic atoms, powerfully burdened

Religious Reactions

the ministerial work of the Church—partly through the uprooting of human beings from a locality, partly through the inner unsettlement it induced. Associative impulses were weakened, to be replaced by collective cement of cash or state. Karl Mannheim has discerned the difference: 'When the mobile person appeared in the market place he behaved more and more as *homo economicus*. When he came in contact with his neighbours in his private life he accepted the ethics of neighbourliness. When he met people with whom he had other social and economic relationships, he changed his tactics with every human contact. Occasionally, a not-too-powerful state forcibly interfered by means of its taxation, police regulations and so on. In private life religion might play a role, and then the contrast between everyday life and holidays became a growing indication of the gulf between these worlds, just as the separation of the office and the factory from the home played an active part in forming a new type of character.'[6] The Church's concern for the break-up of the neighbourly community is not due only to immediate professional considerations; it rests upon conviction that the excessive mobility and change of 'mask' which the individual person has to make in the multifarious contacts of recent times—that these grow to a point at which the human being cannot adapt himself without spiritual and mental and often bodily sickness.

In the third place, capitalism grew up, and its motives almost dominated society, as part of the wave which gave so many secular disciplines their autonomy, their freedom as it were from the apron strings of mother theology. We saw in Lecture One that it also cut adrift economic life from tutelage to the other social and physical realities. The movement by which all economic life became a function of the market mechanism was but the most intense phase of the bigger movement wherein production and exchange of things and energies acquired a life of their own unanswerable to political or national exigencies. And this independence of economic performance was an achievement of a larger tendency still, towards the discovery of a secular sphere of existence with valid laws of its own and no *direct* allegiance to a religious pedagogus. And so it would be easy to argue that because the results of this

Religious Reactions

complete freedom of market economy have been so disastrous, therefore insistence upon the self-reliance of the secular order was itself a calamity.

Some critics, I think hastily, have supposed that was what Mr. Tawney meant to convey. What he did say was that the Church did not work out its ethical and theological teaching on these matters to cope with the new situation created by the break-up of the medieval relatively-closed units and by the beginning of a world market. In default, Mr. Tawney argued, churchmen—aided by the influence of salvation doctrines of Luther, Calvin and the Sects —dropped this sphere of economic behaviour from the department of moral theology—at least in any serious sense. 'It was unnecessary for the Church to insist on commercial morality', he wrote, 'since sound morality coincided with commercial wisdom,' and again: 'In an age of impersonal finance, world markets and a capitalist organization of industry, its (the Church's) traditional social doctrines had no specific to offer, and were merely repeated, when, in order to be effective, they should have been thought out again from the beginning and formulated in new and living terms. ... The social teaching of the Church had ceased to count, because the Church itself had ceased to think.'[7]

A later predecessor of mine in this lectureship, Dr. A. D. Lindsay, as he then was, in his Holland Lectures of 1930 on *Christianity and Economics*,[8] raises this question of the autonomy of secular spheres. He is not satisfied with what he rates to be Mr. Tawney's demand for a recovery of the old synthesis of religion, politics, economics and education. Much gain had been achieved by the separation of politics and government from direct religious sanctions—notably the freedom of the individual. His lectures constitute an argument that an indirect influence of religion on men in an independent economic sphere, not on the economic sphere directly, has the same advantages over the direct authority of ecclesiastical ethics in this sphere—the same advantage as he claims can be seen in the history of politics. 'The new relation,' he wrote, 'because it confines politics and religion to their proper tasks, gives each more scope, but it needs far more faith than an authoritative system. It asks far more of the ordinary member of society and it gives the

Religious Reactions

Church more to do.' Dr. Lindsay has here raised a serious matter. He has not in my opinion stated it quite satisfactorily. For one thing, to approve a development because it asks more of men and gives an institution a bigger job, may be the right attitude when restrictive or lethargic circumstances make for stagnation. But to make it a general principle is too much like regarding life as an obstacle race, the prizes going to those who can erect and surmount the highest hurdles. There are times when the greatest danger comes from situations which have become too much for any human being or institution to cope with. The mind of man is that part of him which can jump quickest; it can set afoot social developments which make it impossible for his whole being and his social organs to handle life with them. As a wise school teacher once said to me of a pupil, 'her mind has gone on much faster than the rest of her'. The question set by Dr. Lindsay's solution of the relation of Christianity and Economics is the very question set to the race of men by the growth of large-scale technical society and its social agglomerations. May it not be that man's powers, used both directly and also in releasing historical momentums which then run on their own, bring about situations which no intelligence, no moral codes, no planning institutions, can order in the human interest? And this, not only because man is sinful and imperfect, not because he hasn't pulled up his socks frequently enough to catch up with his technical and social changes—but because the autonomy of science, economics, politics or education, can be an enriching factor only under certain historic conditions, when there is behind it all an integrating pattern of life as a whole? When the differentiating process eventually quite dissolves the original unity, then the beneficial effects of the differentiation turn to destructive ones. It is not the question whether an authoritative Church should take control again. It is the question whether the autonomy of the secular functions of society can be relied on *per secula seculorum* to serve human destiny. The twentieth century is quite decisively giving a negative answer. This autonomy of the separate spheres must be stopped, it says, sometimes deliberately and with theory to back it, more often blindly and unwittingly in dealing with *ad hoc* emergencies.

Religious Reactions

Dr. Lindsay quotes a discerning passage from one of Baron von Hügel's letters on this subject of the proper autonomy of secular disciplines, as a support for his (Dr. Lindsay's) acceptance of any degree to which autonomy might be pressed. Von Hügel wrote: 'Hence if you ask, "Has not religion to do with everything?" Eucken would answer, "Most certainly!" If "Does it not embrace everything?" he would say "Yes" and "No"; "Yes" if by religion you mean here a notion so all-embracing as to make you respect the various laws immanent to all the various departments of life. "No" if you mean a set of laws or notions which can be taken as the simple regulations and commands of those other laws. Hence religion will have to come to see that it cannot attain to its own depth, it cannot become the chief thing, if it does not continually renounce aspiring after being *everything*; for it cannot become its own fullest self without not merely occasioning the love of the Cross in other departments, but also taking the Cross upon *itself* and then all things will become God for such a faith, and it will become the base and transfigurer of things.'[9] If I may paraphrase this eminent Catholic philosopher, he is saying, encouraged by Rudolf Eucken, that for the Church to allow the various fields of human activity and knowledge to find their own laws and pursue their own distinctive purposes which are not in the specialized sense religious laws or purposes, that is a kind of crucifixion for the Church, but it is the losing of its life to find it.

We shall have to return to this question not only because it is one of first-class theological importance, but also because we have a situation to-day in which the autonomies won by the liberal age are being threatened or frowned upon in the name of social cohesion and economic justice. So totalitarian societies tend to make science and law and business, as well as religion, merely lackeys of one overmastering purpose of social solidarity, real or alleged. This is a danger to the liberties men have struggled for and which in some ways go back to that 'division of powers' inherent in the Christian impact upon human societies.

Again, when the social sciences, in their theoretical and practical aspects, had won their independence of one all-embracing religious conception they soon found themselves impelled to lean on each other for support. Sociology, for instance, at first hastily borrowed its terminology and method from the natural sciences. With Herbert Spencer it began to explain its facts in terms of biological concepts. Society was envisaged as an organism and, with more lasting influence, the idea of evolution was also appropriated. Similarly, Psychology was expounded in terms of Physiology or of instincts, until Freud brought to an end the phase which culminated in the instinct psychology of McDougall and Trotter. In more workaday spheres, politics came to be very much a way of running the economic process; then art and education were judged as assets or liabilities to what was believed to be economic progress. Altogether the sciences tried to unite along their theoretical edges. The attempt was foredoomed to failure, because as each science became more independent it became more abstract, receding from instead of approaching the actual problems of life in the concrete. The attempt lingers in the hope that somehow matter and spirit will be found to have met at the scientific antipodes when physics and psychology have wandered round the abstract world chasing the atom and the soul, away from the one point at which they do meet, human life in its actual setting. It should be added that a more rigid demand for independence in the sciences, beginning obscurely in this century, is renouncing the hasty term-borrowings and spurious analogies which devastated the sociology of the nineteenth.

To return from this not altogether irrelevant digression, the rise of capitalism, taking place as it did, under the sponsorship of the view of the self-sufficingness of the economic realm, presents problems with which any intellectual formulation of religion must come to terms. And then the reversal of this movement, the bending of economic processes to social ends *extra commercium*, sets a question of some historic complexity, because the tendency to overcome the social dissociations is going on when the pre-economic culture which that highly significant development of autonomies presupposes is being so largely dissipated by its enterprising offspring.

It cannot be said that the religious reactions both to the rise of economic autonomy with the market economy in particular, and

Religious Reactions

to the reversal of that independence, have taken hold of the question at the level on which I am expounding it. There is no difficulty in tracking down the reactions on the part of churchmen to the rise of economic individualism. They vary from the serious Calvinist expressions of 'the calling' to the more philistine geniality of Richard Steele who wrote: 'Prudence and Piety were always very good friends . . . you would gain enough of both worlds if you would mind each in its place.'[10] Archbishop Whately could say: 'It is curious to observe, how through a wise and beneficent arrangement of Providence, men thus do the greatest service to the public when they are thinking of nothing but their own gains.'[11]

When we blink at words like those, we should remember that such ecclesiastics were doing marvellously well what the Church is always being urged by its critics to do, keeping abreast of the times and adapting its teaching to the thought of the age. So there is a case for a theology independent of the times! Some of the evidence that men of the Church saw not much deeper than their age is to be found in the last section of Mr. Tawney's book, and in the Hammonds' books: *The Bleak Age*[12] and *The Town Labourer*. Quite clearly that age did not interpret the baptismal promise to renounce the world as including a disentanglement from its assumptions as well as a renunciation of its follies and evils. But there were many isolated and powerful protests in the name of humanity. Mr. Reckitt, in the last Holland Lectures, has made a fascinating story out of the movement of protest in the Church of England; and M. Halévy, in his study of England in 1815, shows how class war was averted by the Methodist Revival—though in the minds of some this should be put down not under the heading of protest, but of condonation. The 'Nonconformist' conscience in England, bound up though it was with the liberal outlook, was one of the first to revolt against the treatment of labour as a commodity.[13] The Roman Catholics with their Papal Encyclicals on social questions and the literature expounding them have produced a large body of criticism of the results of liberalism in economics. If much of this has seemed somewhat theoretical, it has to be remembered that catholic countries have retained much more of non-market relationship in the economic sphere than those whose majority religion was protestant or liberal. Here, for instance, is the case which stimulated Max Weber to make his investigations of Calvinism. An attempt had been made to introduce piece rates in areas where a traditional outlook prevailed. The result was that the catholic women workers in certain sections where the new principle of increasing one's earnings had not yet been realized, stopped their work as soon as they had earned the amount needed for their customary level of maintenance. Even capitalism can function only when it simultaneously creates the corresponding human type which in the earning of money is dominated by the principle of 'more and more'.

On the issues I have tried to draw out of this piece of social history, I will select two statements which show early evidence of a consciousness of them. William Emmanuel von Ketteler, a German Catholic Bishop, wrote in 1869: 'The Physiocrats of the last century' (and he might have added, the classical Economy of his own) 'made the organization of labour responsible for all the economic ills of the people, instead of looking for their true origin in its degeneration, its egotistical ossification and in the patent fact that their organization had not developed to meet changed conditions. And so they annihilated the grand constitution of labour handed on to them from the Middle Ages. . . . This demolition they called restoration of the natural order—*le gouvernement de la nature*. . . . Complete disorganization of the state, of society and of labour; the powers of the state vested in a bureaucratic officialdom on the one side, and on the other the unbridled competition amongst the people dissolved into isolated individuals under the sole control of an absolute monarch or an equally absolute National Assembly— this is the natural law of the revolution. Such, too, is the spirit of liberalism, not merely the spirit of its economic teachings but also of its political and social theories. The tendency of our times to return to corporative forms, far from being a product of liberalism, is on the contrary a reaction against the unnaturalness of its pretended natural law.'[14]

Allowing for a tinge of romanticism in this statement and a tendency to attribute changes too much to the theoretical exponents of a change rather than to see them as wrought by historical forces

Religious Reactions

—allowing for these defects, von Ketteler's point is not very different from that made in the *Communist Manifesto* of Marx and Engels, where we read, 'the bourgeoisie, whenever it got the upper hand, put an end to all feudal, patriarchal, idyllic relations, pitilessly tore asunder the motley feudal ties that bound man to his "natural superiors" and left remaining no other bond between man and man than naked self-interest and callous cash payment'. Again we may put in a caveat to the effect that this is polemic exaggeration, for no society has ever run for a week with nothing but cash economic relations. It is of some consequence to note that, as von Ketteler detected, *laissez-faire* in economics was not incompatible with a powerful bureaucratic state machine.

The other pronouncement I would adduce comes from England and tells another way with regard to the state. It is from Samuel Taylor Coleridge, who is in many ways the fountain head of Christian social criticism of industrial society in England. In 1817 he delivered his *Lay Sermon Addressed to the Higher and Middle Classes on the Existing Distresses and Discontents*. Therein he lays most of the distress of the time to the door of the commercial and credit system. 'I shall perhaps be told', he says, 'that the very evils of this system, even the periodical clash itself, are to be regarded as so much superfluous steam ejected by the escape pipes and safety valves of a self-regulating machine ... that in a free country all things find their level. But persons are not things—but man does not find his level.' Another passage declares: 'There is surely no inconsistency in yielding all due honour to the spirit of trade, and yet charging sundry evils which weaken and reverse its blessings on the overbalance of that spirit, taken as the paramount principle of action in the nation at large.' And this is the chief point he makes: the causes of the distress seem to him 'resolvable into the overbalance of the commercial spirit in consequence of the absence or weakness of the counter-weights.' Mr. Cyril K. Gloyn, whose book on *The Church in the Social Order, a study of Anglican Social Theory from Coleridge to Maurice*, called my attention to this passage, summarizes Coleridge's thesis: 'The growth in influence of the counter-weights —the ancient feelings of rank and ancestry, a philosophical class and religion—has not kept pace with the development of the spirit of trade.'[15] Coleridge's own words are: 'The spirit of commerce is itself capable of being counteracted and enlightened by the spirit of the state.'[16] It looks as if Coleridge is concerned with the spirit of the state in the more organic and historic sense of the fatherland or nation, rather than as the overriding governmental function which Ketteler rightly saw as an aid to the *soi disant* 'natural' free play of economic forces. Coleridge had learnt much from those apostles of nationality in Germany, like the Lutheran minister, Johann Gottfried Herder, whose doctrine of the *Volk* was perverted by the National Socialists a century and a half later.[17]

It was useful to look at a few typical religious reactions to the rise of capitalism, for they raise issues which meet us when we come to assess the religious reactions to its decline. I leave on one side those who defend the epoch of economic competition out of mere self-interest or timid fear of change, or because it still enables church organizations to draw on the accumulated wealth of the community made available by industrialism. We should perhaps in fairness reason with other Christian persons who believe that any system of economic relationships only requires the spirit of stewardship to make it human, oblivious of the fact that ownership under the monopolistic results of the free market, with colossal inequality of economic power—that such ownership cannot be a stewardship, it can only be a dictatorship, as Mr. Reckitt averred many years ago. I leave on one side those valiant Christians who maintain their belief in a 'market economy' because there only, it seems to them, can free enterprise and the pioneer spirit thrive—and are not these things akin to the venture of faith which the Gospel enjoins? Such men are not to be snapped into silence, for they have hold of a truth; but they need to be reminded that the pioneers pioneered in business in order that their children might not have to pioneer so hard and with so many risks; and therefore to fear demoralizing effects of increased security is too much like asking for questions in order to ask more questions instead of for an answer—which typifies so much the kind of religion of keeping on keeping on, gently but firmly parodied in Mr. C. S. Lewis's *The Great Divorce*. They also have to be reminded that there should be enough in the realms of the spirit to give exercise to the pioneer impulses if it is wanted, without the scramble to find and keep a place in the economic system. To-day, however, it looks as if the spirit of enterprise will be called for in a new direction. If society is to offer increased security, it cannot neglect the need for repeated obedience to laws of the universe which operate in the earth's life, in community and in the realm of the spirit; and that obedience is to the man of the modern world so much against the grain that submission to it is a kind of pioneering.

To get another objection out of the way, Christians have no business to be resisting the suppression of the free play of economc forces by more collective movements on the ground that these are materialistic. For one thing, they are materialistic largely (if that is a fault in the eyes of a religion of the Incarnation and Resurrection) because they are heirs of the same materialism, or virtual atheism, as the forces of developing capitalism were. This is not to say that men in bourgeois society were all materialistically minded or atheist; it is to say that the theory which justified the capitalist experiment and regarded it as the fulfilment of humanity, and the view of man which it took for granted, were at variance with the Christian conception of the world and the human being. Besides, every human action and every historic movement, whether its attention is directed to material facts or the Kingdom of Heaven, is a spiritual phenomenon. For human life is distinguished from the rhythm of Nature only because man is a spirit-centred organism. He can only hold a materialistic creed because he approaches the physical substratum of things from a vantage point outside it.[18]

Now, we can turn to our main concluding considerations. In so far as the outlook which gave autonomy to the secular spheres, when it worked out to its most intense artificiality in the marketableness of all economic factors—in so far as this is inimical to man, in the estimate of the Christian mind, both for reasons of doctrine and because of its effect on men, then, it might be asked, is not the great reversal of all this just what Christian advocacy should support? That would be delightfully simple and I should have no more to say. For the rest of these lectures are to discuss the complexities arising out of that question with the hope of disentangling some of them. The main point here to be emphasized is that the great reversal—the various protections society is producing as antidotes to the disintegrating results of autonomous economic processes—that reversal is not embedding economic life again in the whole social organism from which the Enlightenment emancipated it. What the decline of capitalism is making for is not what the rise of capitalism made away from.

First of all, when we are seeking to judge the force, validity and fidelity to Christian truth, of movements and epochs, any identifiable period has to be seen as having not one but several layers to it, and those layers may represent different complementary and sometimes opposing principles. And movements which seek to change or overturn existing or previous structures are often informed, in another layer of their existence, by the same assumptions as those obtaining in the disfavoured past. It is these assumptions common to two contending positions which are most frequently regarded by the devotees of each as part of the natural order. We will now use this realization of different layers in a period, to see the source of much confusion about the religious reactions we are endeavouring to understand.

The period of capitalism, as we may call the latter half of the eighteenth and most of the nineteenth century, has much else in its economic and social structure besides the free interplay of marketable commodities and services. Underneath that, and keeping society together, were ties and responsibilities surviving from the feudal and local social structure. Underneath it, too, were dispositions and spontaneous social disciplines reared in towns and localities, small enough to constitute what the sociologists call an 'assessment group' where every member is under moral and social assessment by his community fellows. That wisest father of modern sociology, Frederick Le Play, and his disciple Emile Durkheim, as well as experts like Karl Mannheim, have made clear that only because of this non-capitalist sub-structure, was the market economy possible on top of it. We considered earlier how the virtues which produced the pioneering spirit of capitalist enterprise were those engendered by the communal sense and asceticism of an earlier period—and that the product dissolved its own primary ingredients. There was also much religion and the ethics of Christianity informing persons in the capitalist era—and much unpaid public service. Many of these survivals have been all but destroyed by the march of economic and technical society.

When men, therefore, compare this immediate past with the present or with what they see of the near future, unless they distinguish various layers they take one or other over-simplified attitude. Seeing the liberal age in a lump they see it before the commercial and technical organization has eaten too far into the organic foundation. Then they say it was not so destructive a period as the present; they attribute the destructiveness to the forces transforming the liberal economic age into a collectivist economic age, whereas the disruptive forces do but continue at a deeper level what was started in the period revolted against. Or, such observers, aware of elements of stability and natural community in the growing and most-developed period of capitalist industrial economy, attribute this element of health to the free play of pecuniary and trading motives, whereas these could achieve a certain independent life and considerable productive success only because they stood on what they inherited. There are to-day some schools called the 'Edward the Sixth Schools'; they are so called not because he founded them; they are the schools Edward VI did not destroy. Similarly, the things we often see when we look back to the great capitalist era—the unities grown out of kinship, neighbourhood, craft, profession and faith—the soil out of which all society, however enterprising, must grow—these are the things which capitalism had not yet destroyed, though it was in process of doing so.

Another possible error arising out of the failure to distinguish levels in an historic period is the habit of attributing the inhuman and dissociating effects of the free-market economy to what is in fact the opposite principle of rootedness which informed the less conscious foundations of that age. Thus, socialist critics are inclined to call 'capitalism' all that preceded the present revolt against it.

Again, you may argue that society is now succeeding in varying degrees in bringing economic forces under social direction and control—subordinating the principle of gain to that of social solidarity as a determinant of value—and that therefore this reversal is a recovery of natural community relations or a stage on the way thereto. This erroneous deduction ignores the same phenomenon of varying layers in a social configuration. The transition from unimpeded monetary motives in economic life to such things as state ownership and direction of production and trade, protection of employment whether it pays or not, and incomes partly independent of earnings—in brief, to controlled economy—this transition represents a change in economic organization.

However great that change in organization, it takes place within a common factor of social culture which had already given the new society a structure quite unlike that of the past. We may call this new structure and its culture, which is common to both capitalist and socialist phases, by the name of Bourgeois Society, in spite of the determination of socialist analysis to confine it to the former. It is true that a number of the earlier socialists in England, like William Morris and John Ruskin, hated this bourgeois culture and hoped that the transition to socialism would replace motives of monetary gain, commodity hedonism and mere technical expediency by a spirit of neighbourliness concerned with man's higher faculties, artistic interest and production done for its own excellence. Such a hope was soon discouraged by the actual trend of socialist movements which everywhere, with insignificant exceptions, seemed bent upon socializing the structure and culture which the capitalist age had inaugurated. So it came to this. On both the liberal and collectivist sides of the transition there were operating the same forces affecting the cultural patterns and social relations of men. These forces were at variance with those which capitalism had inherited and with which it lived and on which it counted, in spite of the contradictory principles in what capitalism was making for and what it was standing on. The culture and dispositions of the bourgeois society steadily displaced the inherited ones, and it has had to wait for its second phase—namely the socialist phase—to see them almost completely disappear.

The social historian, if his sweep is wide enough and his insight deep enough, is bound to be more impressed by the similarity in style of capitalist and socialist society than by their organizational

Religious Reactions

differences. He is more impressed by the contrast between industrial culture in both its phases and that of mankind during most of its history than with the apparent similarity of the capitalist age to its predecessors. He sees that this alleged similarity is made to appear a real one, both by a polemic socialist interest in identifying all pre-socialist forms of society as equally exploitative, and by a more general confusion of two things which overlapped one another for a time until their incompatibility worked itself out in the victory of economic, contractual and mere citizen relationships over the older domestic, hierarchic, local and status groupings.

In order to estimate whether the forces of dissipation or recuperation are the stronger in the transition, it is necessary to look behind the differences of economic and political organization which distinguish capitalism from socialism. Such an estimate can only be reached by assessing how far bourgeois society can stand on its own feet, even with the crutch of state collectivism, after it has all but destroyed the pre-economic social bonds.

It is possible, in the light of this preliminary examination, to see why some of the main religious reactions to this complicated bit of social history often seem to have an ambiguous and changing character. In the period of the rise of capitalism there were, as we have noticed, two religious voices. One accepted the philosophy of the new economic system and acclaimed it to be a reflection of Nature as ordered by the Creator. This voice also admonished men to take their lot submissively. 'Christianity', wrote William Wilberforce, 'reminds the lesser orders that their more lowly path has been allotted to them by the hand of God; that it is their part faithfully to discharge its duties and contentedly to bear its inconveniences; that the present state of things is very short; that the objects about which worldly men conflict so eagerly are not worth the contest ... and finally that all human distinctions will soon be done away.'[19]

This attitude, it has been justly pointed out, might have some validity in the simple frugality of a settled community, but amid the scramble of the transition to industrialism 'there could hardly be a more disastrous way of commending spiritual truth to a population'. It is an attitude taken over from a pre-market age where fidelity in one's status had some cogency, and it was then applied to a different condition where submissiveness was against the tenor of an epoch—an epoch in which prosperity was the prize of economic enterprise and where neglect to rise in the economic scale incurred the penalty of remaining among the submerged proletariat. But there was sufficient of the pre-industrial pattern still surviving to give this attitude some moral plausibility and to explain the confusion.

On the other side, the Hammonds, whose chapter on Religion in *The Bleak Age* is critical enough of the clergy, point out that many a parson and magistrate spent his days in debating remedies, and how in the 'forties 'The Vicars of Leeds, Bradford, Wakefield, Huddersfield, Dewsbury and of many smaller towns, acted as chairmen regularly at meetings for the Ten Hours Bill. . . . The Church paper, the *Guardian*, gave strong support to the Bill.' (The Factory Act of 1847.)[20] There was another apparent ambiguity in the religious reactions to the later developments of capitalism. Methodism, in the early nineteenth century, while sponsoring the motives that made the industrial age, also provided by its own religious fellowships a substitute for the more organic unities of earlier periods.[21] Evangelicalism has thus at the same time been harshly judged for accepting the social relations of capitalism and complimented for being in M. Halévy's phrase 'the moral cement of English Society'. Then, again, churchmen who were opposed to 'the reforms' of radicals like Jeremy Bentham were moved to their opposition by a realization that both the industrial development and the reforms which purported to humanize and liberate it from feudal shackles, were tarred with the same rationalist and utilitarian brush. 'The Church of England,' writes Professor Greenslade, 'especially in its bishops, was against the latter (social and parliamentary reform) wrongly but sincerely, for the bishops could have won an easy popularity by voting for it in the Lords. Early in the century, while, as we tend to forget, England was mainly agricultural and most of the clergy still lived in the country, the Church wanted to protect agriculture and feared concessions to the manufacturing interest. It could not line up with the Benthamite prophets of industrial progress.'[22]

Religious Reactions

In the same half of the century, Coleridge, Thomas Arnold and the Oxford High Church Movement stood for a reaction against individualism through their emphasis upon the organic and historical character of society. In their implied criticism of purely economic and contractual bonds they anticipated the 'socialism' of the later nineteenth century.[23] The ambiguity of the situation is seen in the fact that these men and movements were considered 'reactionary' by the growing industrial and commercial interests and by the radicals who were beginning to misapply the doctrines of biological evolution to the history of societies. Had Marx and Engels been aware of these religious forces they would no doubt have named them under the heading of 'Reactionary Socialism' which they gibed at in the third part of the *Communist Manifesto*. A similar situation has arisen in the twentieth century when the inroads of industrial and trading economy dissipates the tribal order and social cohesion of native peoples. African bishops told me in 1948 that when they voiced their genuine alarm at the uprooting of Africans by the supplanting of native society by commercial and wage relationships, along with monetary taxation, they were answered: 'Oh, you are reactionaries; you are trying to keep us back.' Perhaps socialist criticism of capitalism could have stood on stronger ground, endured fewer intellectual confusions and suffered less emotional ambiguity, if it had admitted that socialism was a reactionary movement, and the better for that! As it is, it has attached itself to an evolutionary or progressive ideology, and in consequence seems chained to a kind of historic determinism which makes it necessary to give societies the capitalist disease before it can administer the socialist cure. And perhaps it is socialism which will universalize the bourgeois culture whose capitalist organization it set out to supplant.

In the middle of the last century when thinkers were still making straight moral and social judgements about the trend of events, without the later attempts to be scientific and wrap their judgements in the guise of social evolution or dialectical inevitableness, there was no embarrassment in linking pre-capitalist norms with post-capitalist aims. The new State Philosophy, of which the Factory Act was the overt symptom, was widely acclaimed as a

Religious Reactions

correction of recent tendencies—it harked back to a norm which had been departed from. Among English churchmen there was plenty of testimony in this direction. Frederick Denison Maurice, writing in 1848 and 1852, declared: 'I must have Monarchy, Aristocracy and Socialism, or rather Humanity, recognized as necessary elements, as conditions of an organic Christian Society.'[24] Here we have the expression of a view which can link some of the pre-capitalist features of society with the adumbrated post-capitalist state philosophy of the future.

A more specific question was the proletarian condition of the worker who was gaining economic freedom while losing security and status. By the dissolution of all claims upon society except those he could purchase with his wage, he tended to be left with nothing on which he could count as a right; everything had to be earned by selling the labour power which was inseparable from himself. The evil of a proletarian loss of status was a main count against capitalism made by Marx and the early communists; but the condemnation of proletarianism was taken up later by the Guild Socialists who numbered many churchmen and who unsuccessfully sought to divert British labour from state collectivism to the recovery of authentic artisan status through industrial corporations. There was a strong Christian protest, if not very widespread, against the entire dependence of livelihood upon the price that labour would fetch, as if labour were but another completely marketable commodity. This found utterance in such statements as this one of J. M. Ludlow's, the barrister who in fact inaugurated the modern Christian Social Movement in the Church of England. 'The condition of the wages receiver is not to me an ideal for the worker. It is a sort of washed out slavery.'[25] Then there was Bishop B. F. Westcott who, addressing the Church Congress of 1890, said: 'Wage labour, though it appears to be an inevitable step in the evolution of society, is as little fitted to represent finally or adequately the connection of man with man in production of wealth as in earlier times slavery or serfdom.'[26] It is noteworthy that Westcott, like Marx, was so much a child of his age that he could not help confusing his moral judgements by bringing in the notion of inevitable steps in the evolution of society.

Religious Reactions

It was this sense of the iniquity of rootless men having only their bodily labour to bargain with which led some churchmen to welcome a movement which would restore to men some status as citizens which they could not attain as functioning members of the community. 'The State must take up her neighbourly responsibility', wrote Scott Holland, 'or it can never be taken up at all. But this is Socialism, you cry. Exactly. This is the irresistible verity on which socialism has seized.'[27]

This faith that 'the State principle' would restore the social bonds which a hypertrophied market principle had weakened continued to inspire an influential group of churchmen as well as many secular idealists. But after 1914 it began to appear that it was not so straightforward to equate the 'State principle', coming on top of capitalism, with the real social principle. Confidence in state collectivism became more guarded and hesitant, even among those who saw no other way to accord justice and status in economic relationships—a concern which all the Churches voiced with a painful conscience in connection with the tragedy of wide-scale unemployment. New and serious considerations were being raised which obscured the over-simple alternative of market economy or state socialism in the minds of Christians who gave thought to these things.

For one thing, it appeared that collectivist economics were being tried out under some of the assumptions of the capitalist period, assumptions which seemed inimical to the moral stature and social needs of men and to the reproduction of the real economic basis of all systems. Here was the same encouragement to motives of commodity hedonism; the same reckless dissipation of man's estate; the same impulse to over-develop the technical side of life at the expense of the biological, community and spiritual substance of society; the same arrogance of industrial nations which disregarded their agronomic foundations and expected the rest of the world to provide them with food and raw materials on their own terms; the same economic rationalism holding that state-planned prosperity in place of enterprise prosperity would content the human being and bring out his native associative impulses; the same perfectionism which believed that now at last

Religious Reactions

human life had found in organization the solution of its inner conflicts.

The realization that these tendencies were not confined to a free-market economy but would be furthered under collectivist régimes, opened up questions not of this or that organization of industry, but of the nature of industrialism itself. Some tendencies which began under capitalism appeared to shoot up with greater force with the succeeding collectivist trends. Not only capitalist society but the whole bourgeois culture in both phases seemed to be suffering from contradictions within it. The socialist aim, based on the same radical hopes with which capitalist enterprise had been imbued, was founded upon a certainty of unceasing all-round wealth, the superior wisdom of popular government and the greater peacefulness of democratic politics. History was beginning to shake these certainties. The modern economic man brought up with sublime confidence in the power to arrange his own destiny in the world, finding the hopes of a whole epoch thwarted, suffered the feeling of a sharp slap in the face. There grew imperceptibly a sense of homelessness and purposelessness in the economic age, and for the more thoughtful this raised a doubt whether the whole of Western culture had any future. A weakening of points of support in marriage and the family, in local autonomies and in corporate responsibilities in areas of life smaller than the state, took place between the bleak alternatives of bare market relationships or bare citizen status, and insinuated a cryptic resentment against things in general. As the resentment became more acute, it was projected with greater bitterness against class opponents, foreign peoples or upon one's own national community, leading to a widespread fifth-column mentality.

Problems like these pressed the religious consciousness which was directed to such matters, to penetrate to a deeper level than that on which the organizational struggle between capitalism and socialism was being staged. Some of the issues they present will occupy later chapters, but this one may fittingly conclude with a general statement of three specific reasons why the decline of capitalism calls for religious concern and interpretation.

In the first place, capitalism was in theory associated with individualism, and so its decline is in practice making for the total state. The transition from one to the other has made clearer to the religious mind that the principle of the omnicompetent state and the myth of the self-sufficient individual are both twins of the same parentage, that of naturalist humanism which distils from human life in its biological, community and spiritual setting, the two abstractions of individual and state which the reason can encompass. The significant contrast is between the historically grown associations held in a loose unity by a state responsible to a higher principle on the one hand, and absolute individualism or absolute *étatisme* on the other.

Then, secondly, the Christian Church has a stake in a society where there is a plurality of powers, not chiefly because the Church must have her own warrants apart from the realm of Caesar; mainly because only when social power is divided—by constitutional recognition and by strong vitalities in the domestic, professional, artisan, and intellectual functions—only then is the person sufficiently free from overwhelming social pressures to pursue his religious, artistic and scientific purposes for their own valid ends. It was not socialism, it was capitalism that began to disintegrate these counterweights to the state. But this process goes on under collectivist auspices.

The third serious factor in the age of transition is this: capitalism and early socialism were informed by the clear rationalism of the Enlightenment. Whitehead, in *Adventures of Ideas*, makes plain that this rationalism, as it affects Europe, came from the medieval scholastics' refurbishing of Greek rationality. Because this rational handling of life at first made obeisance to the organic, non-rational, super-rational realities it could win many triumphs. When it took over most of the field, or sought to do so—and did this under the banner of freedom—then it was found that this freedom gave rein not only to reason but also to the dark forces in man and community. We have what has been called the *Return of the Demons*, the uprush of irrational powers.

Religion could handle these and so make possible the liberation of reason, but reason itself cannot subdue them. So in this crisis of our time Religion and Reason are on the same side.

Religious Reactions

NOTES

1. K. Polanyi, *Origins of our Time*, p. 139.
2. For these quotations and others *vide*: W. Stark, *The History of Economics*, pp. 74 and 75 *et passim*.
3. *Principles of Political Economy* (ed. Ashley, 1909), pp. 199 ff.
4. *The Economic Theory of the Leisure Class*, 1927, p. 49.
5. R. W. Church, *Occasional Papers*, vol. II, p. 386.
6. *Man and Society* (London 1940), p. 161.
7. *Religion and the Rise of Capitalism*, p. 192 and 184, 185 (Pelican ed., pp. 177 and 171).
8. A. D. Lindsay, *Christianity and Economics* (London 1933).
9. Quoted in Lindsay, op. cit., p. 28 ff.
10. *The Tradesman's Calling*, quoted by Tawney, op. cit., p. 245 (Pelican 220).
11. Whately, Political Economy (1831)
12. J. L. and Barbara Hammond, *The Bleak Age* (Pelican), p. 116 ff.
13. cf. chap.: 'Non-Conformity and the Working Class', in H. F. Lovell Cocks' *The Non-Conformist Conscience* (Independent Press).
14. *Die Arbeiterfrage und das Christentum* (Mayence 1864).
15. C. K. Gloyn, *The Church in the Social Order* (Pacific University 1942), p. 17.
16. *Lay Sermons*, pp. 402, 403.
17. It is noteworthy that the *Communist Manifesto* accepted the Economic Man to such an extent that it declared, in direct contradiction of Herder and his followers: 'The Workers have no fatherland.'
18. It is not socialism but capitalism that created *homo economicus*, as Berdyaev was always saying.
19. W. Wilberforce, *Practical View of the System of Christianity* (1789), p. 314, quoted in C. E. Hudson and M. B. Reckitt, *The Church and the World*, vol. III (1940), p. 7, from which the following comment is taken.
20. *The Bleak Age*, p. 201.
21. cf. E. Halévy, *History of the English People*, vol. III, pp. 166 ff.; G. M. Trevelyan, *English Social History*, pp. 492 ff.; and J. L. and Barbara Hammond, op. cit., pp. 130 ff.
22. S. L. Greenslade, *The Church and the Social Order* (1948), p. 105. The book is an excellent historical sketch of what the Church throughout its history has done in respect of the social order.
23. For this period, see C. E. Hudson and M. B. Reckitt, *The Church and the World*, vol. III.
24. In letters to J. M. Ludlow, quoted in *Life of Frederick Denison Maurice*, vol. I, p. 484; vol. II, p. 131.
25. 'A Dialogue on Co-operation', *Economic Review*, 1892 (vol. II, pp. 214–30), quoted in C. E. Raven, *Christian Socialism*, p. 249.
26. Quoted in M. B. Reckitt, *From Maurice to Temple*, p. 144.
27. Quoted in D. O. Wagner, *The Church of England and Social Reform since 1854* (Columbia University Press, U.S.A.).

CHAPTER III

Aims and Axioms

★

'Why the Liberal Era could do without Religion' is the heading of a section in the late Professor Karl Mannheim's *Diagnosis of Our Time*.[1] His explanation is that a liberal and competitive economy and its society can function quite well with neutralized values as long as there is no threat from within or without which makes a basic consensus imperative. He adds: 'It is not a matter of chance that both Communism and Fascism try to develop and superimpose a pseudo-religious integration in order to create a psychological and sociological background for planning.' Mannheim's concern is that 'democratic' societies shall not succumb to attack from totalitarian régimes, and therefore that these liberal communities shall be integrated on those deep levels on which religion integrated pre-industrial societies. It is arguable that this eminent thinker has not contributed much guidance in this task because he has not satisfactorily answered his own question: 'Why the Liberal Era could do without Religion.' It is not much help to say it survived until threatened by rivals, for the rivals to the liberal society arose because of its enfeeblement. The rivals are two: the non-liberal, tight, unitary systems which arose within the area affected by the age of liberalism, partly in protest against and partly in fulfilment of the mechanization of culture; and, secondly, the rise to power of Slav, Eastern and other peoples who have never passed through the liberal experience but are now using many of its intellectual and technical results.

The answer to the question why the era of philosophical radicalism, of political liberalism and economic free enterprise could do without religion is that, in a sense, it didn't. We have already glanced at the cosmological deism of the hidden hand and the ethical doctrine of the identity of interests. The fact is that what Mannheim calls *neutral* values were that which the representative figures of the liberal outlook believed to be a residue, belonging to man and Nature as such, when the traditional, supernatural and ecclesiastical beliefs of a particular historical period had been discarded. The remainder of such a subtraction sum is, however, not Nature, but the aims of a tradition without its axioms. These aims live on for a while until they are displaced by new aims more in keeping with the new axioms that have replaced the discarded axioms.

Before illustrating this proposition, I call attention to one of the fullest treatments of the debt of the liberal age to the traditional, classical and Christian past against which it revolted. It is to be found in the works of Mr. Christopher Dawson, especially *Progress and Religion* and *The Judgement of the Nations*. From the latter take this passage: 'When we speak of the followers of the new religion of progress as "pagans" we are using the word in a different sense from that of the ancient paganism. Locke and Franklin, Rousseau and Lamartine, J. S. Mill and Guizot and de Tocqueville were a great deal further removed from paganism than were their medieval ancestors. They were indeed still Christians of a sort, even though they no longer believed that they believed. To-day this type of sublimated Christianity is discredited. In fact it has been the object of a sharper and more intense criticism than dogmatic Christianity. It is easy to understand that this change has been welcomed by pious Christians as a sign of religious revival and of a reawakening of religious faith. It is, however, nothing of the kind. It simply means that the disintegrating movement which was first directed against institutional and dogmatic Christianity has now been concentrated against the Christian ethos and the moral and humanitarian idealism that was derived from it.'[2]

We considered in the two earlier lectures how the capitalist phase of the liberal age presupposed the social structures inherited from the ancient and medieval world; that it counted on the

Aims and Axioms

solidarities and dispositions thus inherited as if these would always be there. These were not therefore thought of or talked about. We might say they were part of liberalism's unconscious. On top of the organic, civic, domestic and craft society was reared the tremendous superstructure of economic enterprise, political democracy, intellectual exploration and technical mastery of natural forces. It never occurred to the leaders in this achievement that the foundation they were counting on might be dissipated by the very weight of the superstructure. They were, as we all are in our various situations, so excited about what they were standing for that they assumed the permanence of what they were standing on.

In a similar way, the aims of the liberal era, which informed much of the capitalist spirit, came out of a definite historical period which preceded it. In that historical period those aims stemmed from a certain culture, and largely forming that culture were a number of axioms about the nature of things. The modern age gradually discarded these traditional axioms, but it retained the aims that had been reared upon them. It steadily repudiated the dependence of the aims upon their proper axioms and considered the aims as part of the *humanum* as such, the very structure of human life in its bare essence. That is to say, it attributed to Nature what were in fact the highly specialized moral and social products of a peculiar historical and cultural achievement. We still live to a large extent in the climate of that mistake. Moreover, on the eve of the modern age it began to be held with passionate conviction that these aims, which we may roughly gather under the heading of Humanism, needed a new set of axioms about existence and new institutions and devices, in order to make them more effective in human life. It was not suspected at all that a change in the axioms, in the *Weltanschauungen* (as the Germans call them), in the things taken for granted about the structure of existence—that a change here might in the end falsify the aims and make them look absurd. It was not until the twentieth century that this result began to be seen.[3]

The distinction and relation between aims and axioms is an important clue for understanding social change. The aims which characterize a period as well as an individual, are the views men

Aims and Axioms

have of the good life, the things they want to be and do, the possessions they want to obtain, the system they want to live under—in short, a desirable state of affairs to be worked for. The axioms, in the context in which I am here using the word, are the presuppositions men have about the nature of things, their unquestioned outlook concerning existence, the unformulated certainties they take for granted as to what the world and man and history are. Axioms may be formulated in doctrines which are the subject of teaching, discussion and proclamation. At their most influential they are, however, not formulated at all but assumed as the datum from which all formulation and discussion proceed.

I am arguing that the human and religious significance of the changes marked by the rise and decline of capitalism can only be discerned by realizing that the aims of a period are sometimes backed up with axioms which are congruous with those aims, in which case there is a vitality and robustness of cultural growth; and sometimes aims are still held when the axioms have changed and men have not yet displaced the older by newer aims. There is then cultural weakness and, in its extreme form, disintegration, however tenaciously the aims are still held. It is necessary, however, to state that the more hidden and less conscious forces which may support or may conflict with the aims of a period, include other things besides the axioms. The axioms are part of the mentality of a culture and the most hidden part of its mentality. But along with its mentality there are other deep forces which form a culture and give a certain bent to its soul. There is, for instance, what we may call its 'rituals', the things individuals and classes of men do every day or in other regular ways: their work, their recreations, casual spare-time occupations—in fact, any fairly recurring scheme of living. These things, much more than their prevalent ideals, tend to mould men's feelings, attitudes, fears, hopes, loves and hates. Besides these 'rituals' there is the order of importance and values men accord to different kinds of person and occupation—their estimates of various jobs, interests and aptitudes, which affects their views as to what is a step up or a slide down the social scale. These three influences, the axioms, the 'rituals' and the social valuations, largely form the soul of a period below the level

Aims and Axioms

of men's religious, artistic, intellectual and political pursuits. For the purposes of this lecture we must confine ourselves mainly to the axioms or dogmas involved, while inquiring where the aims and the axioms of the period we are considering may harmonize or conflict with each other.

What, then, have been the aims of our Western, democratic, liberal culture? They have been the enhancement and extension of certain values which had marked the civilization of Western man. The Enlightenment and Liberal Radicalism did not invent them but sought to give them a universal sway. This they attempted by devising entirely new philosophies and social structures. Briefly, the aims of liberalism have been to embody in life and thought the truth that while man is a social being he does not exist merely for the social whole. He has certain valid human goals, such as the pursuit of knowledge, the creation of civilization, the exercise of each one's proper skills, the enrichment of personal life and relations, and the fulfilment of spiritual destiny.

Liberty was the banner under which marched all the great attempts to extend to all men the opportunity of following these purposes. On this banner were inscribed a number of subsidiary liberties which make up the larger liberty; concern for one or other of them received varying emphases in different phases of the liberal era. Such were freedom of thought and conscience, freedom to own and acquire property, freedom to get on in the world, free access to the provisions of justice, freedom to resist pressures of others. Behind these departmental freedoms, the main concern of liberal thought and policy was to provide protection against the bias of governments to judge all human activities by their amenability to the sole purpose of social solidarity. It was seeking to embody the principle that to sacrifice valid personal aims for the sake of collective cohesion, if it comes to that point, is to pay a price that barters away what is essentially human in both the person and the natural groupings of mankind. This is the origin of the specifically political aspects of liberalism. It was expressed by John Stuart Mill in the well-known passage from his treatise, *On Liberty*: 'There is a limit to the legitimate interference of collective opinion with individual independence, and to find that limit and to maintain it against encroachment is as indispensable to the good condition of human affairs as protection against political despotism.' A more recent writer puts it this way: 'Freedom exists in a State when a man knows that the decisions made by the ultimate authority do not invade his personality.'[4]

It is now clearer than it was in the past two centuries that the personal goals to reach which Liberty was struggled for, were an historical product and not in human existence as such. Because they are to-day threatened by anti-liberal philosophies and régimes, we discover that the aims of liberalism were an inheritance from a culture and not part of the natural human scene. We may list four of the main objects of the liberal faith which have been so much ingredients of our Western culture that they could easily be mistaken for what is given with man at all times. First comes the pursuit of truth. This assumes an objective reality about things that can be grasped and ought to be sought for by eliminating bias and cultivating disinterestedness. It relies upon the human mind being able to disengage itself from the relative position in which each inquirer finds himself and to stand clear from all that makes his concrete situation in the cosmic flux a unique and irrepeatable one. This possibility has been challenged by such critics as Marx and Nietzsche and those who proclaim the sociology of knowledge. They insist that our apprehension of truth cannot be objective but is always determined by our sociological situation and our interests. Undoubtedly such a tendency has been airily neglected by an over-confident belief in the naturally independent powers of the mind; but it is a salutary corrective only because it seeks to free us from the deception of confusing our prejudices with the truth. Science has proceeded, in the days of its ascendancy, on the principle that the personal factor which introduces an element of bias can be weeded out. The aim of passing from a subjective self-orientated attitude to an objective and disinterested one is the opposite of the view, now appearing, that there can or must be no truth, scientific, cultural or religious, that is not propaganda in some form or other.[5]

A second aim of liberalism was the recognition of a certain rightness and wrongness as a universal criterion by which men and things and events could be judged. The moral distinction was to be open to all to see by themselves and to legislate for; it was no longer to have its source in any authority, civil or ecclesiastical. It is true that the early liberal thinkers fell short of making this a universal criterion in practice and that later ones encouraged an attitude of relativism in ethics. Yet the liberal principle assumed on the whole, along with traditional outlooks, the notion of an absolute good and evil, even though actual codes of conduct are relative and often misleading applications of this notion. Right and wrong have a metaphysical force and are not merely serviceable conceptions in the struggle of life. The good is an attribute of a certain kind of life and cannot be identified with life itself or with the bare success of an act. This meant that there is something worth dying—that is giving up life—for. That something is the rightness which the thought of civilized life has called the good.

For liberalism the free society was self-evidently an embodiment of the good, and it had thus its moral law which was superior to any ordinance of state or church. Man does not, therefore, surrender his conscience to society, for society is free only in so far as it respects his conscience; exercise of that conscience is the purpose of freedom. The duty of giving up life for the good, if needs must, applies to any part or the whole of the collective as well as to the individual life, a doctrine which is not satisfied by the sacrifice of the personal life for the sake of communal survival. Now, the decline of liberalism has been marked by the uprush of doctrines and policies which reverse all this, and which make ethics a view serviceable to action instead of a criterion of action. Modern absolutist collectivist systems use the idea of a universal good merely as 'a monkey trick' to gain support for the naked interests of a sectional group in its striving for survival or power.

In contrast to this anti-liberal reversal of the ethical premises of our culture, the common ground in liberal and traditional acceptance of ultimate universal moral standards can be recognized, in spite of liberalism's establishment of them on its own new philosophies. The same ultimate and universal character of the good which historically had a transcendent and theological basis was set by liberalism upon a historical or psychological foundation. So

Aims and Axioms

we find the doctrines of liberalism deriving the good from such premises as the general will, or greatest happiness, or the harmony of interests, or utility; or assimilated to the Newtonian law of universal attraction; we find the good reposed upon a presumed sympathy in man, as in Hume, Adam Smith and Bentham, or benevolence in James Mill. We find attempts like Jeremy Bentham's to establish morals upon the model of the deductive sciences, in order that morals may keep their universal character, as when he rejects all 'anarchical' principles, namely those from which derive 'as many standards of right and wrong as there are men'. In others we find the good life needing a political instrument in the division of powers and also requiring individualist and equalitarian outlooks. In short, what the liberals hoped to foster on a basis of reason, experience and changeless human dispositions, was the same 'laborious art' of ethics which before had depended upon a religious tradition or innate principles. They sought to fulfil the goal announced by Francis Bacon in the *New Atlantis*, namely 'the service of human convenience'.

In the third place, we may glance at the legal extension of the moral assumptions, which constitutes another aim of liberal thought. Here the aim was to secure that the positive laws of particular states and legislatures were not treated as absolute and that they should be dependent on the constitution of reality—sometimes called Natural Law or Natural Rights. This goes back to medieval ideas that the law is above the ruler who is the instrument and not the source of law. The ruler is subject to a universal justice; he interprets and administers it; but his will does not create it. The law is therefore something to which the subject can appeal against a decision of the ruling authority. This recognition of a law of human ordering is the expression of the conviction that persons have a certain priority over institutions. There is, in the last resort, a common right or reason upon which the person can rely if his personal fulfilment is opposed by the demands of the institution. Notwithstanding all the difficulties in giving this principle a political application, it remains the source of the limitation of state power and of 'the rights of man', and of the separation of the judiciary from the executive. And it is the denial of the recrudescent

Aims and Axioms

doctrine, becoming prominent to-day, that legal decisions are intended to promote the actual policy of the ruling power and nothing else.

The fourth aim which, in stages, became of eminent concern for the leaders of the liberal age was the recognition of a certain universal common character in all human beings. This element, common to all men by their very nature, merits a proper moral respect and legislative protection. It lies behind all differences due to behaviour, or to racial, national, class or sex variations, and behind the relative position each holds in the social organism or the function he performs. This element of man's being does not come out of man's social relationships but is brought into them, and it therefore constitutes a bond between men over and above their membership in the corporate body. This common element has been the foundation on which later liberals grounded their equalitarianism. But inequality is inherent in man as a natural and functioning part of the social order, in the family, in politics, and in industry. Therefore if man's significance is confined to his place and purpose in society, there can be no equality and no common element in the inner being of all men. So it is by virtue of men standing in relation to a reality over and above their concrete place in social history, that men can speak of 'our common humanity'.[6]

These are but four of the more general aims of men in the liberal era. It was the purpose of leaders in that era to further the attainment of those aims by what they thought were appropriate new theories and social machinery. These aims became conscious as social principles through the movement of emancipation from ancient and medieval outlooks. But they are outgrowths from elements in those outlooks and depend upon a great many assumptions, habits and social patterns which have been swept away in the modern humanist age. The grand interest of the liberal age was to establish the status of persons free to pursue personal goals apart from their serviceability to institutions. This interest grew to heightened self-consciousness in the modern period after it had been nursed by a long tradition beginning with Greek rationality which stood back from the flux of all things to ask the reason why,[7]

Aims and Axioms

and perhaps earlier still in the very fact of human language.[8] It received its mightiest impulse in the Judaeo-Christian dogma or axiom that this and that creaturely thing has its being and its significance from its relation to the Creator and not only as an item in the world process. In so far as this doctrine of the significance of particulars, as distinct from their being part of a whole, is an element in the liberal outlook, it derives from a pre-liberal dogma which liberalism proceeded to reject, namely a two-dimensional view of existence—the two dimensions being: one, the relation of this creature to the rest of its immanent context and, two, its relation to the transcendent ground of existence which for the Bible is the High and Lofty One that inhabiteth eternity.[9]

When liberal doctrine asserts that the pursuit of truth or goodness or beauty or justice or skill constitutes a greater loyalty to what is permanently in the human interest than the cohesive power of any existing social structure, it rests upon two axioms which have been worn away in the career of modern liberalism. One is that persons find their true being by embodying in the temporal order the absolute permanent values of the eternal order, and the second is that the social order in its political or cohesive aspect is subordinate to this personal purpose. The liberal doctrine amounts to the claim that the human person is the mediator between the eternal law and the social order; the anti-liberal doctrines of the twentieth century affirm that the social reality is the mediator between the eternal law and the human person. This totalitarian claim cannot be withstood on the dogma that man is only part of the world process, for in that context only he is nothing but a smaller part of the cosmic flux than the tribe, state, class or nation.

The genuine religious outlook has always understood existence as constituted by an eternal world behind and related to the temporal world; it has held that the fact of process which marks everything in the temporal world is given a meaning by reference to an abiding, transcendent source of being which, though not itself in process, is the origin of all things and the key of their destinies. Religions differ in the way they regard this particular relation of eternity and time. For Christianity it is expressed in the doctrine

Aims and Axioms

of Creation in which each part of the creation has its meaning from the source and not ultimately from its relation to the world. Living parts of the universe like man himself, his histories, communities and actions, are significant in themselves in relation to the divine Will and Purpose and not only because they participate in the whole world process. Christianity has pressed this insight still further. It made the relation of each man to the eternal God a precise relation to the person of Jesus the Christ, in whose flesh the eternal irrupts into time. He is the second Adam, the republication of the origin of all things: He appears, dies and rises from the dead at 'the end of the times'—anticipating the end when history will be wound up and its meaning fully disclosed. But on any view of life in this double dimension of eternity and time, man has his peculiar significance from the fact that he stands in a unique relation to the eternal, while at the same time he is involved in the process of the earth's life and the sweep of human history.[10]

One other axiom which the liberal age presupposed and which it accepted as the heir of the Classical-Christian Western culture is that the whole world has a unity but the principle of its unity transcends the world process. This is the ultimate basis of the possibility of the coincidence of order and liberty, which has marked that culture. The recognition of a substratum of unity behind all things is the presupposition of science and of universal political principles. But if this source of unity is conceived to reside somewhere in the immanent order, in the cosmic process itself, then there can in the end be no liberty, for all things will be tied inextricably to the function or place where it is thought to be. That is why the doctrines of autonomous spheres of knowledge and of the political division of powers have their roots in the world outlook of traditional European man and nowhere else.

It is the argument of this chapter that aims which liberalism presupposed have their origin in axioms which its age inherited of the stock of human outlooks from earlier periods, and that men in the liberal age sought to sustain these aims with a new set of axioms. And this is the cause of the decline of what is positive in the liberal aim and doctrine. The aims have begun to lose their hold on men in the West and are openly threatened by counter-doctrines because their fulfilment has been sought on the basis of a dogma, an axiom, at variance with those which gave them their greatest stimulus. The new axiom was at bottom that man's existence is only in one dimension, that of the world process. He is a drop in becoming; he has no roots in being, behind and above. And, of course, if he is but a drop in the stream he has no rights against larger rivulets in the stream of becoming, such as the race, the state or the economic system. The totalitarian claim to man's soul in the name of one of these larger currents of the total stream cannot be resisted on this dogma—at least not with that conviction that one is backed by the structure of reality, which is required in the major crises of history. Hence what was true *sub specie æternitatis* in the liberal aim is being lost through the working out of an alien axiom, the dogma that all reality is process. An examination of the main theories of the liberal age reveals that in them the good life at which it aimed was expounded in terms of the immanent order, first one aspect of it then another. Reason, nature, economic desires, each had their champions. It is also in this period that we had certain total explanations of human life in terms of one or other of its functions; there was a succession and rivalry of such dogmas of the essential man as the rational man, biological man, economic man and political man. The absolute, dethroned from Heaven, was insinuated into some aspect of the sub-lunar world.

In the capitalist period, as I have repeated, these aims of the liberal era were taken for granted as permanent attributes of man, and as inherent in the immanent process, whereas they were an inheritance from a specific culture. In the decline of capitalism we see that the historic revolts against the market economy of capitalism and the culmination of purely immanentist outlooks in some collective absolute, have become conjoined in a vast reaction against the liberal idea. This is to be expected, for the axioms of a period, even when for a time they allow aims derived from previous cultures to survive, eventually become clothed with their own kind of culture which then tends to encourage other kinds of aims for human life. When there is a conflict between the aims and the culture out of which men act, in the end the aims will be displaced so that the collective soul of man may be healed of its division.

Aims and Axioms

That is how I account for the decline of the liberal idea; its aims clung to with so much devotion and pertinacity are being defeated by the liberal axiom that man is merely part of a process. The decline of capitalism is due to certain contradictions within it which should have been detected had not men been misled by an immanentist dogma of reason as something inherent in the world process, whereas it is an instrument by which man does things with the world process. Now, we can with this interpretation of aims and axioms account for the inability of the Christian conscience to take a simple Yes or No attitude to the decline of capitalism which is one of the critical aspects of the decline of liberalism. Such an interpretation accounts for the frequently observed fact that men's collective aims turn into something else, often at variance with them, just when they seem to reach fulfilment. That is why society of the twentieth century is not at all what the men of the nineteenth century meant to produce. Here is an example from another sphere to illustrate this deflection of aims. Brought up in one of the northern industrial towns, I learnt much in the first two decades of this century from workers who had at great effort made themselves an education with such aids as were given, largely voluntarily, by the more leisured. These men had imbibed something of the European tradition or what used to be called its liberal culture; they read their Greek drama or their Ibsen; some had learnt philosophy and history; they could talk Plato or Emerson. And they reasoned thus: if we with a struggle have done these things, how good if all citizens at an earlier age, as part of their schooling and after, were at least put in the way of acquiring this background. So they pioneered for universal education. And when we got this universal education on a compulsory basis—that is not what the young are being taught. What they are being taught apart from technical aptitudes is not easy to see. The point I am making is that the aims of those old men as I knew them have turned sour on them.

There is an excellent treatment of the weakening of the liberal humanitarian ideal, expressed in a different idiom to mine, in the earlier chapters of A. N. Whitehead's *Adventures of Ideas*. He points out how 'at the moment when the "brotherhood of man" triumphed, the intellectual world was meditating on political economy conceived in terms of unrestrained competition, on Malthus' law that the mass of the population must always press on the limits of bare subsistence, and the zoological law of natural selection by which an iron environment crushed out the less-favoured species, and on Hume's criticism of the notion of the soul. This new trend of thought was in its immediate origin British and is to be compared and contrasted with the antecedent Wesleyan movement. In neither case did the leaders intend the sociological effects which followed from their efforts. It is often the case that the originators belong to the antecedent epoch, and stand outside the epoch of their followers.'

Any interpretation of human affairs which claims to use the Christian doctrine about the nature of existence, must perforce recognize that this recurring problem of the deflection of men's aims and their thwarting is the religious problem as described in the Pauline account of salvation. We all know the experience of being caught out in behaviour the exact opposite of the way in which we intended to meet a situation. The situation of his own inner life is set out by St. Paul in the seventh and eighth chapters of the Epistle to the Romans. He did not require the Gospel to give him good aims; they were his as a good Pharisee. It was to cope with 'the other law in my members warring against the law of my mind' that he found it necessary to accept a force from outside him, the grace of God, to unite these two parts of his soul—for more intensive willing only made his ineffectiveness worse. Which is to say on the religious level what we can discern from the ups and downs of history, that aims require support by the culture of the soul or of society; and prominent among the forces which form a culture are the axioms men hold without knowing that they hold them—their unformulated dogmas. The ups of history mean that the culture backs up the aims; the downs of history mean that while the aims may still be high ones, the forces underneath pull the other way.

To dwell a little further on this psychological apparatus for understanding the vicissitudes of great movements of the human race: M. Coué some years ago said, among several silly things, one

Aims and Axioms

wise one: 'When there is a conflict between the will and the imagination, the imagination always wins.' The terminology has been questioned, but the point stands. The images which inform our minds, especially those we accept as showing what reality is like, will always overcome aims which may assume a different pattern of reality.

And now, one more consideration before applying this relation of aims and axioms to the situation of capitalism in its rise and decline. Professor Herbert Butterfield, in his study of *Christianity and History*, has given his own interpretation in terms of a Biblical anthropology of the way in which men's corporate efforts in history, like the personal goals, are deflected or defeated. He speaks of this falsifying force as human sinfulness and the judgement it incurs. This is correct from a Christian point of view. But he has used the image of a 'gravitational pull' to bring out the character of this deflecting force, picturing a projectile aimed in a certain direction but drawn downwards away from the target to the earth. Now the analogy of a gravitational pull can have a different force, as it did in a figure used by Luther. Unredeemed mankind is, he says, like a drunken peasant; when helped up on to his horse on one side he immediately falls off on the other. That is gravitation all right, and it accounts for one-half of the human predicament. The other half must be accounted for, namely in this illustration why the peasant is not always lying on the ground, why he wants to get on a horse, why drunkenness has to be invoked in order to explain why he doesn't stay there, and why he could ride the animal if he were sober. Which, being interpreted, means that a fully religious interpretation of human affairs has to account for the aims which get deflected as well as for the deflection, and to throw some light on the recurrent pursuit of purposes by which men seek to find a fulfilment of their life in that tricky sphere of human affairs outside the cradle of Mother Nature—a pursuit taken up again after every colossal failure.[11] This is a pointer to our final lecture. In taking notice of it, it is worth recalling that Augustine, our first Christian interpreter of history, uses the image of gravity, not for the force which deflects but for the force which makes men have aims—that is the force by which they go out from

Aims and Axioms

the regular and somnolent cycles of Nature. The restlessness of man is a kind of *pondus* or weight which moves him towards the centre of gravity. This is God the Creator exercising a continual pull upon His creatures. In this image man's enterprises are his search for centrality—the deflections are the pull of outer layers of his existence seeking to be treated as the true *centrum*. The fallenness of man is a kind of tragic eccentricity. The Church has put this fact into an intellectual formulation in its doctrine of the natural law or *Lex Naturae*.[12] This conception, adapted from the Stoics, has from the point of view of the moralist, been traditionally presented as a set of norms and standards, and so long as Christendom grew its own culture, it was sufficient for it to have an ethical force only. When that culture can no longer be counted on, this *Lex Naturae* has to be seen as also an operative force, pulling man away from one false position towards his *centrum*. But, because of the alienation between human existence and its created purpose, mankind, like Luther's drunken peasant, makes for an opposite false absolute. Only conscious response to the natural law will bring fulfilment of life.[13] This *Lex Naturae* is personified as Wisdom in the eighth chapter of Proverbs.

Now, this force which the theologians call the *Lex Naturae* means that which appertains to the nature or essence of human life, and is not to be equated with what we now call Nature, for this Nature is that part of reality which remains when the transcendent God and the human spirit which transcends Nature are left out of account. That which appertains to the *natura* of man (and I shall use the Latin term to distinguish from Nature) includes the link between human existence and the eternal God as a bare fact— without necessarily that consciousness of the link and response to it which is religion—it also includes, that is to say, what makes man more than an item in the cycle of Nature or a drop in the stream of history. The force by which he is alienated from his true *natura*, and from the divine source of things, is a perversion of the spiritual mobility he has as something made in the image of God with *His* freedom over His creation.

These anticipatory considerations are a required preliminary for seeing the meteoric career of capitalist society and its sequels,

Aims and Axioms

in the light of Christian understanding of history. Every movement has in it these deforming forces—the evil in it; but it has valid impulses too, as well as the egoism and power-striving of one set of people overreaching others. The valid impulse need not always be a genuine universal concern for mankind as such; it may be the support it gets through the moral disguises it assumes, for no movement can acquire power without at least the appearance of a general aim for the good of man. Hypocrisy is the tribute vice pays to virtue. If you will re-read E. H. Carr's *Twenty Years Crisis*, which represented a tough realism bidding us recognize the factors of power-striving in international politics, you will find an emphasis too upon the need for power to assume the appearance of a universally moral aim for the fulfilment of all human life on earth. Moreover, every large turn of modern history has been supported by a faith that it runs along the grain of universal purpose itself—that it is according to the nature of things. In the centuries following the Renaissance this first took the theological form of a deism for which Providence set the works going and kept them going by an infallible mechanism, though it could be mightily hindered by the parts which had the obstinacy to be reluctant. In the later phase of the modern period the reference to Providence was dropped without much difference to the outlook, and then all the forces concerned were thought of as operating within the world order only—it was a dogma of pure immanence. And on this view there was no fundamental contradiction in man; the dialectical movements of which I have offered a sketchy diagnosis were thought of as operating in one linear dimension. There were only two possibilities, going on or pulling back, the nature of things pushing man towards the goal if only he would follow on and not be a stubborn, tiresome pull-back; or else he was offered the rewards of following his immanent reason if he would use it to overcome his involvement in all that was behind him. The axiom that man is only part of the world process led to reading into Nature his most ingenious achievements. One of these achievements was the development of the ethical and political pattern of European society; a further result was the highly intellectual notion of independent spheres of life, autonomies as we have called them. In the economic part of existence this reached its climax in the idea of market relationships as the substance of economic life. We may say that this represents a high degree of abstraction or generalization, a product of the civilizing faculties of Western man, for, as Whitehead said in *Modes of Thought*: 'Civilized beings are those who survey the world with some large generality of understanding.' Because this separating out of exchange and contract relations was regarded as the latest heave of the cosmic flux, instead of a pattern imposed upon it by the spirit of man, the whole career of industrial commercialism was informed by some questionable assumptions. For example, it was not suspected that free enterprise once started could be killed by its very success in creating vast conglomerations of economic power which exercised monopolistic domination; it was taken for granted that large-scale production would always employ the labour and capital available; that markets would always be found for the products of industry, and that the money mechanism would always reflect and not interfere with the meeting of demand and supply. These assumptions are challenged by socialist criticism.

But there are other assumptions shared by upholders of free enterprise and collectivism alike. Such as, for instance, that because technical methods and large-scale production have served many human needs their benefits are in direct proportion to their extent; that because life has been enriched and variegated by division of labour and specialization between areas, therefore every extension of them or continuance under changed conditions must add to the advantages and can never be socially disintegrating; that there can never be too much production and trade because human demands are insatiable or can be made so; and that man will always sacrifice other satisfactions for economic ones. These and many other unquestioned premises spring from the axiom that the direction taken by industrial society in its early stages is part of the natural process of things. Therefore it was held that the benefits accruing up to a point must logically be increased by going all along the line. Such an outlook ignores the fact that in the social texture of human life the scale of things alters the effects which seem inevitable to mere quantitative logic. We shall have to look at

Aims and Axioms

this again when we consider our situation as a vicissitude of civilization.

Let us look for a moment at the background of these assumptions. Never was there such a cocksure confidence as in the early modern period that man had found the secret of fulfilling his life. Listen to Descartes: 'I perceived it to be possible to arrive at a knowledge highly useful in life—and to render ourselves the lords and possessors of nature.' Listen to the President of the Royal Society in 1702, Thomas Sprat: 'And we may well guess that the absolute perfection of the True Philosophy is not now far off, seeing this first great and necessary preparation for its coming is already taken off our hands.'[14] It was in this spirit that the upholders of the free market in all the elements of economic life contended that it was according to Nature. It must be allowed that they had not the evidence now available of the customs of simpler communities which show the exact opposite. But their *a priori* construction of natural man as an economic exchange wiseacre could only have become a matter of conviction by force of an overriding dogma—for in their concrete treatment they allowed that the natural state of things had to be assisted. 'Competition was often artificially fostered by mercantilism, in order to organize markets with automatic regulation of supply and demand,' wrote E. F. Heckscher, the historian of mercantilism.[15] There is an interesting passage in Adam Smith's *Wealth of Nations* which is but one example of the need for special measures, by state and other directive powers, to make the alleged self-regulating market system work freely. He admits that the extreme division of labour which the free market presupposes tends to make the labourer as 'stupid and ignorant as it is possible for a human creature to become. . . . His dexterity in his own particular trade seems in this manner to be acquired at the expense of his intellectual, social and martial virtues. But in every improved and civilized society this is a state into which the labouring poor, that is the great body of the people, must necessarily fall, unless government takes some means to prevent it.'[16] M. Halévy comments: 'It becomes necessary to restrict the bearing of the principle of the natural identity of interests and to say: the interests of all individuals are identical, provided that the indivi-

Aims and Axioms

duals know what their interests are; it is a function of the state to teach them to know what they are';[17] and in another passage he adds: 'One of two things must be true; either the thesis of commercial and industrial liberty is really derived from the principles of the new school of political economy, in which case it does not imply the natural identity of interests; or else it does imply this spontaneous identity of the interest of each with the interest of all, in which case the thesis of economic liberalism is not derived from the principles on which Ricardo based his system.'[18]

It seems then that *laissez-faire* was an artificial construction assisted by the state, and that economic liberalism assumed the state to be the instrument of restoring man to his natural condition. What caused him to depart from it? The answer was easy: evil traditionalism. That was about as far as thought went; the dogma of progress was just assumed. There is a remarkable speech of Richard Cobden's to the National Freehold Land Society in 1849 which has much good sense; in it he says this: 'the plan (that of giving men a plot of ground to qualify for the franchise and augment their wages) was a practical mode of effecting a great change in the depository of political power in the country; for he avowed that he wanted, by legal and legitimate means, to place as much political power as he could in the hands of the middle and industrial classes.' So there had to be political action. But then comes his naïve assumption that the international self-regulating market is in the law of progress: 'Why! At the present moment . . . the agricultural members were thinking how they could restore protection. Why—these men must be the disciples of the inquisitors of old who put Galileo in prison because he said that the world turned on its axis, and in like manner these, their modern disciples, insisted that the moral world should not roll on.'[19] This bland assumption may raise a smile to-day. But there was a consistency about it, the lack of which has weakened so much of the socialist counter-movement to the automatic play of the market in Western Europe and America. I refer to the inconsistency of requiring protection within each society, of labour, money and land from exploitation by a free-market economy—to protect these foundations of life by subordinating market considera-

Aims and Axioms

tions to non-economic needs—and then to suppose that between nations and areas trade must find its own level, that it be free in a multilateral market. That is perhaps an irrelevant interjection of mine at this point, but it does provide another example of the fatal ease with which men take for natural, that is belonging to the structure of things for always, what they have imbibed from a tradition (in this case the very recent tradition of free trade) inimical to their aims.

We must look for a moment at evidence for an analogous tendency to assume the permanence of specialized moral dispositions and congruous social structures, regarding them as inalienable from human life, to confuse them with *natura* and expect them to exercise a corrective influence through every aberration. Take for instance Adam Smith himself, who did as much as any man to give a rational foundation for the emancipation of economics from religious or ethical control. He wrote not only *The Wealth of Nations*, but also *The Theory of Moral Sentiments*. He recognized that a society which dispensed with super-economic regulations had to compensate for it by seeing that its members were subject to some internal rules of self-restriction, for even economic man is to act within the limits of 'justice' and self-command. Moreover, he believed that 'sympathy' with others was an integral element in man's nature; reason would proclaim this and thus offset the harshness of a naked pursuit of interest. Again, his philosophy assumed the small-scale society where men, even adversaries, can be known and met, and where social discipline is largely exercised by spontaneous approval and disapproval. Jefferson in America too championed the free society, believing that the soberness, conscientiousness and responsibility of men endowed with the puritan conscience were part of man's inalienable character. Bentham and Auguste Comte, to quote but two others, both took the ethical idea they had inherited from the European tradition as part of Nature. These examples typify the error of the liberal age. It was not their aims that were wrong; it was their assumptions about existence. This so largely accounts for the shortlivedness of the capitalist phase, for it strung up to the highest pitch, in the economic sphere, a freedom which can only flourish on top of non-economic bonds that make for community cohesion, and assumed these to be indestructible. The very success of a self-regulating market in economic gain disintegrated the non-economic bonds underneath. It is the rise, not the decline, of capitalism that requires explanation as a very special development. Professor Dicey, in *Law and Opinion in England*, infers, to his surprise, that measures for social control against the free play of market relations were spontaneous *ad hoc* measures, and not, in the last century, the result of counter-theories. I am told that more measures in the direction of state administration of economic affairs were put through under conservative (*alias* liberal) governments than under socialist ones. Mr. Karl Polanyi has some grounds for his dictum: '*Laissez-faire* was planned, planning was not!' The Decline of Capitalism is in fact ultimately due to the pull of man's total *natura* away from one of the most ingenious but ultimately unstable fabrications of the human spirit. But the situation presented to the religious consciousness by its decline is full of complication not out of concern for theological precision, but out of concern for the truly human interest. To put a previous question again, will the whole of the liberal idea have to go down, with its positive contribution to man's existence, with its sources in the spiritual supremacy of the human being over his context, with its mainspring in the Christian doctrine of man's link with God and the division of power within society and not just between the earthly and the heavenly—will all this have to be renounced because society refuses to allow contract economic relations in a free market to dominate it?

Let us lay open this question a little further. We shall be handicapped if we suppose that prior to the contemporary decline of capitalism, there were only two main types of economy: the free-market one which dominated, though it did not completely possess, the preceding era, and the one before that, the medieval and city economy described by Tawney, Pirenne and others. It is necessary to appreciate that this pre-capitalist society in which economic processes were a matter of ethics and legislation coming, as they did, under the heading of *justitia*, was a highly developed form of city and agrarian society which covered a good deal of the civilized world since classical times. This town economy and its

Aims and Axioms

mutuality with the barbarian landsman outside the city (and the conflicts between these two) and then the regulation of buying and selling, money transactions, guild discipline, and other features of medieval society—this whole thing was itself an innovation. It may possibly have been a high-water mark of man's *natura* coming to self-consciousness, but it certainly was not Nature. For when man is nearest to Nature his economic life is an indistinguishable part of his tribal existence; it does not have to come under positive law, for such law has not arisen; there is little exchange in any commercial sense, certainly no motive of gain. The anthropologists' evidence is plentiful.[20] In the more developed economy of the ancient city states and medieval Europe we already reach a high degree of sophistication, there is the beginning of the dissociation of economic life from biological and religious functions, although the whole conception of *justitia* is the product of a religious civilization. The obloquy in which cupidity is held in medieval ethics is a sign that the dominant economic relations of mutuality were liable to serious damage from an incipient commercial spirit which was widely known from antiquity. But the non-capitalist dispositions formed the main character of this stage, and they survived into our own century. Max Weber started off on his whole inquiry into the origin of the capitalist spirit stimulated by the observation that quite up to the present many communities agree that the opportunity for earning more is less attractive than working less. 'A man does not ask how much more can I earn in a day if I do as much work as possible, but how much must I work in order to earn the wage 2½ marks which I earned before and which takes care of my traditional needs.'[21] This pre-capitalist spirit must not be confused with the prudence of this very time which brings about the same reluctance to work harder after careful rational calculations about the inroads of the tax collector. Nietzsche wrote, nearly a century ago: 'The artisans of the south are not industrious because of acquisitiveness, but because someone is always coming who wants a horse shod or a carriage mended. . . . In a fruitful land he has little trouble in supporting himself, for that purpose he needs only a small amount of work, certainly no industry.' The need to induce the motive of gain is one of the disastrous necessi-

Aims and Axioms

ties arising from contacts of commercial civilizations with natives. 'To maintain a community in which the accumulation of goods is regarded as anti-social', wrote Clark Wissel of a West Indian tribe, 'and integrate the same with contemporary white culture is to try and harmonize two incompatible institutional systems.'[22] The tribal institution is in a way pre-economic in our sense of the word and has a certain internal toughness in consequence. Mosca, the Italian sociological writer, mentions some Polish serfs who put up with terrible economic deprivations from their overlords until these masters started imitating the French in speech and costume. In spite of the masters' adoption of radical humanitarian ideas, the workmen felt that their superiors had deserted them, they could no longer rely on him to protect them from their enemies, defend their faith and represent them to God.[23] There we have the tribal solidarity paramount and all other considerations, economic ones too, subordinate. It is the resurgence of this tribal solidarity, in revolt against the abstractions of the economic age, that is the deepest urge behind modern nationalism. But tribal togetherness is perhaps one of those things which must survive in some layer of society for any developed set of purely economic relations, either capitalist or socialist, to be more than an ephemeral phenomenon. In their remarkably wise earlier chapters of *The Bleak Age*, John and Barbara Hammond show how in the societies of the ancient world, where trade began to flourish, the main social element was non-economic. Even behind much strife there was in Greece the moral influence of common possessions and the practice of social fellowship stimulated by the spectacle of beautiful buildings. Public beauty, common enjoyment and voluntary associations formed, until it decayed, the social substance of this culture which had made civilization by transcending a purely tribal life. The Hammonds go on to point out that in the modern industrial age the one thing that reconciled men to their social uprootedness, the thing that in this society took the place that common enjoyment had taken in the ancient world, was the prospect of individual success. 'Men could rise by their own merit and their own effort. . . . The man who in other ages wished to follow in the steps of Wolsey had to put on the cassock of a Church, but a Peel or an Arkwright

Aims and Axioms

could become a millionaire without the surrender of conscience or freedom to anybody's keeping. This was the novelty that fascinated men like Cobden.'[24]

When the unreality of this ideal as a possibility for all men becomes manifest, the decline of capitalism has set in. Our problem can now be stated in these terms. Between tribal society, with its livelihood-getting, its mutual gifts and its division of labour as due only to biological and social differences of function, without exchange in any economic sense—between that and the capitalist age where social order tends to become an appendage of market economy—between these two occurred the civic and agrarian society of the ancient and medieval worlds. It was in this intermediate phase that the germinating principles of the personal society were sown. The Renaissance and Reformation marked a stage when the personalist and pluralist tendencies in the new great society of Europe were given a push that went far to separate the new freedoms from their matrix in the social substance of life. Capitalism represents the extremest form of this emancipation in the economic sphere.

Social history seems to prove that the deeper the human crisis of an age, the further back it has to look to find the forces of recovery or the deeper in the layers of human culture. So we can restate our central question: Will societies involved in the decline of capitalism be able to overcome the socially disintegrating forces of independent motives of economic success, without losing the positive, human, and spiritually created achievements of European culture, that is to say without finding itself plunged into a new tribalism? This is a religious crisis of the first order.

NOTES

1. Karl Mannheim, *Diagnosis of our Time* (London 1943), p. 101.
2. Christopher Dawson, *The Judgement of Nations* (London 1943), p. 13.
3. I dispense with a full exposition of this relation between aims and axioms, for I have enlarged upon it elsewhere. The conflict between the aims and the culture of a period are treated in my opening lecture of the series *Our Culture:*

Aims and Axioms

Its Christian Roots and Present Crisis (1947), and the incompatibility of the aims of Liberalism with its dogmas about reality is the theme of an earlier work, *The Religious Prospect* (1939). Some paragraphs which here follow are to some extent a summary of the exposition given in these two works.

4. Harold Laski, *Liberty in the Modern State* (Pelican Books), p. 63.
5. For a scientific use of this presupposition, see the important work of Karl Mannheim, *Ideology and Utopia* (1939).
6. Jacques Maritain has described this metaphysical and moral equality which does not negate the concrete and useful inequalities in men or make them appear equal only by envisaging an abstract humanity divorced from real persons, in his essay, 'Human Equality', *Redeeming the Time* (1943).
7. cf. Edwyn Bevan, *Christianity and Hellenism*, pp. 14-15.
8. cf. R. A. Wilson, 'Language introduced the element of permanence into a vanishing world.'—*The Miraculous Birth of Language* (Guild Books 1941), p. 154.
9. cf. S. Kierkegaard, 'Man is a synthesis of the temporal and the eternal,' *Sickness unto Death*, chap. I; 'The individual is superior to the universal . . . (he) determines his relation to the universal by his relation to the absolute, and not his relation to the absolute by his relation to the universal,' *Fear and Trembling*, chap. II; 'Earthly and worldly anxiety is rendered possible by the fact that man, compounded of the temporal and the eternal, became a self,' *Christian Discourses*, chap. VI.
10. For further emphasis in Christian thought on the significance of particulars, see the author's *The Religious Prospect*, pp. 43 ff.
11. For this theme, see the drama, *The Tragedy of Man*, by Imri Madach, an Hungarian playwright (Institute of Slavonic Studies).
12. cf. R. Hooker, 'The Law of Nature, meaning thereby the law which human nature knoweth itself in reason universally bound unto, which also for that cause may be termed fitly the law of reason. This law I say comprehendeth all those things which men by the light of this natural understanding evidently know, to be becoming or unbecoming, virtuous or vicious, good or evil for them to do.'—*Ecclesiastical Polity*, Bk. I, viii, 9.
13. I have more fully presented this diagnosis in *The Religious Prospect* where the swing-over from a false individualism to an equally false collectivism is described in such terms, as also the reaction of irrational vitalism to the desiccating sway of purely rationalist accounts of existence. I have also treated of this idea of a 'Natural Order' in a chapter of the composite volume, *Prospect for Christendom*, reprinted in *Theology of Society*.
14. *History of the Royal Society* (2nd ed. 1702).
15. E. F. Heckscher, *Mercantilism*, 1935.
16. *Wealth of Nations*, Bk. V, chap. I, pt. III, art. ii (ed. Cannan 1930 vol. II, pp. 267, 268).
17. E. Halévy, *The Growth of Philosophic Radicalism*, 1949, p. 248.
18. Ibid., p. 370.
19. R. Cobden: Speech at inaugural meeting of the National Freehold Land Society held at the London Tavern on 26th November 1849, as reported in *The Times* of 27th November 1849. Reproduced in Appendix III to *Bricks and Mortals*, by Sir Harold Bellman, *The Story of the Building Zone Movement* (1949).
20. cf. R. C. Thurnwald, *Economics in Primitive Communities* (1932); B. Malin-

Aims and Axioms

owski, *Argonauts of the Western Pacific* (1930); V. A. Demant, *Exchange among the Food Gatherers* in *Christian Polity* (1936).

21. op. cit., p. 60.
22. Clark Wissel, Introduction to Margaret Mead's *The Changing Culture of an Indian Tribe*, 1932.
23. G. Mosca, *Elementi di Scienza Politica*. Selected translation, *The Ruling Class*, 1939.
24. *The Bleak Age* (Pelican ed.), p. 49.

CHAPTER IV

The Political Faiths

★

'We have been turned out of Paradise.' This has been said to us again recently, not this time by a Church father, but by Lionel Robbins, who is a Professor of Economic Science. He explains: 'We have neither eternal life nor unlimited means of gratification. Everywhere we turn, if we choose one thing we must relinquish others which, in different circumstances, we would wish not to have relinquished. Scarcity of means to satisfy given ends is an almost ubiquitous condition of human behaviour.'[1] For him, the fact that men cannot have all their wants gratified and must give up some satisfactions in order to have others makes the human situation that gives rise to economics. That is correct, if it is not assumed that all choices which determine economic behaviour are choices exclusively between economic satisfactions. But the suggestion that the necessity of renouncing this for the sake of that satisfaction is the substance of man's alienation from his supreme good is very doubtful theology. It calls attention to the finite and conditioned character of all things in this world. Christianity, however, has never taught that the limitations of man's terrestrial life constitute the fall of man, as some of the Oriental and Greek religious philosophies have held.[2] Limitation and finitude are aspects of the created order and are not in themselves the principle of evil or unfulfilment. The fallenness of man consists in a certain net of evil in which mankind is caught because of his refusal to live obediently and strategically with these limitations; because of his succumbing to the seduction to 'be as gods'.[3] And there is then a secret hope that by overcoming the limitations of

The Political Faiths

his creaturely existence, man can thereby undo the chains forged by his rebellion.

But we *have* been turned out of Paradise, and it still has enough hold on us to make us want to bring it on earth in our own way. That helps us to interpret the situation we now come to deal with.

But first a few words of recapitulation. We saw a kind of fate at work in which the independence gained by the secular spheres from religion and ethics led at one stage to the bending of social purposes to economic ends; and then how all economic considerations tended to become adjuncts of the free play of market forces. We did not stay to look for an inevitable logic connecting these three steps, but we considered two largely unsuspected factors: one, that the whole development was a productive and commercial success as long as it rested upon a pre-capitalist layer which it eventually ate too far into to survive; another, that before this process reached its climax human nature was protecting itself from social dislocation by various socialistic measures.

Not only did men believe that the substructure would always be there, they also held that the aims of the liberal age for the flowering of personalities were part of the trend of things and that they would be realized for man considered an item in the world process. In the last lecture I pointed out that these aims of giving status and significance to particular things, persons and associations in their own right and not merely as contributors to a larger whole—namely what was positive in the liberal idea—these aims derived really from the opposite axiom that human existence stands in another dimension as well as the temporal one. It has roots in a source of meaning behind the flux of things; otherwise the part has no claim to be left unswallowed by a bigger part of the whole. Otherwise there would be no theories of life, only life itself; otherwise there would be no judgements about the good and bad in history. Christian thought affirms this two-dimensional frame by saying that human life, while it is involved in Nature and history and conditioned by them, has links in its very being with the Eternal God who transcends the world as well as operating within it by His immanent action. The nature of man includes the link between human existence and the eternal God as a bare fact—

without necessarily the consciousness of that link and response to it which is religion. In addition Christianity affirms that man has a mobility, a power to round on his source—a capacity to handle reality by thought, a freedom to say 'yes' or 'no'. This power is the image of God in him, a kind of delegated replica of the freedom of God over His creation. It is a metaphysical and not necessarily a moral image for this makes man neither holy nor blessed—as Ruysbroek would say—it merely makes him man, and gives him the power to become a devil.

Let us look again at the different picture in the outlook of the recent past. In all movements which change the historic situation, men usually support their efforts by a faith that their aims are in the trend of a universal purpose. We have seen that in the earlier phase of the modern period this found a theological expression in the doctrine of a Deity who inaugurated the mechanism of development and kept it infallibly in operation from above. It could not, therefore, be defeated, though its progress could be hindered by reactionary forces of human perversity.

This deist doctrine meant that the human world could not be in any serious contradiction to the universal purpose, and that it would run along its predestined lines without the need of repeated re-submission to the divine will. When, later, the theology was dropped, the same process was conceived in purely immanentist terms, but the outlook was not much altered. With such an outlook there can be no accounting for the colossal defeat of the great hopes of the epoch.

By contrast, this other picture of these things, drawn from a Christian interpretation of existence, does, I believe, provide a more penetrating insight. The human situation at every point is the result of an interaction of two forces, man's link with the place of his origin and place of his fulfilment which Christians call God, *and* his alienation from it. The alienation is not due to his being a finite, earthly, limited and historical creature, for he is these things by creation; it is due to the propensity in him to give some aspect of his relative and limited existence an absolute and infinite value. It may be his mind or his spirit, then he follows the sin of Lucifer; it may be his possessions, or vital urges, then he seeks to relapse into the stream of Nature, fleeing from the pain of individuality. What a bliss that would be! Or it may be one valid part of his communal life—like his race, or state, or class or economic devices—that is assumed to be that which gives significance to all the rest. To repeat, this propensity to make absolute and universal what is relative and conditional is the blind or wilful working of the fact that at the root of his being man is tugged at through his link with the unconditioned, namely that he is the kind of creature the Christian religion says he is.

In the age of capitalist economic enterprise, as we have seen, its achievements and devices were regarded as universal, belonging to man as such. This axiom was followed by others: that one layer of human society, the economic one, was the substance of social existence; and further that the market relations were central in the economic sphere. Now, to pursue the diagnosis I am trying to present, when absolute value is given to a relative construction of human spirit, or when something valid but peripheral is treated as central, then sooner or later men are pulled by their very nature and often without awareness to correct the misbalance and seek to live by a counter-principle. But this too is off centre. And so long as men see their lives only as part of the immanent order, the new principle is treated as central too or given the value of the lost Paradise. So, for instance, periods of rationalism give place to more vitalistic dogmas; idealism to materialism and the other way round. We are now about to consider the swing-over from the market principle to the state principle. All these are ways in which man is pulled from one eccentricity by the cord that holds him to the place of fulfilment, and because he is at the same time alienated from it by seeking it in the sole dimension of his terrestrial existence, he goes over to another eccentric position. Moreover, all the vultures of egoism, power-striving, pride and self-deception, gather round this transformation and make full use of it. Of course, they deck themselves in the moral feathers plucked from the simple-minded doves who only know that the change is seeking to overcome the previous evil. The good which strives against this one evil becomes mistaken for the original or ultimate or final harmony of things, and thus arise colossal idolatries, oppressions and terrible sacrifices of persons for an alleged ultimate fulfilment.

But short of these extreme results, on a less catastrophic plane, other things happen which in my view can only be understood with the kind of diagnosis I am suggesting. The one we are now ready to scrutinize is the move away from the kind of misbalance represented by economic and market relations as the constitutive principle of society, to the state principle as the substance of community. This is a marked feature of the great reversal which we have loosely called the decline of capitalism.

When I say that the state principle is replacing the economic principle, I mean that the political fact of the modern state becomes the most conscious instrument by which peoples seek to recover community after the breakdown of market economy. In fact, it is only in the lands of the more developed political tradition—what we roughly call the democracies—that the state stands for the primary social bond in the minds of most people. Elsewhere, in Europe and the East, where the claims of the social whole are pressed most thoroughly and ruthlessly, the state is regarded as an instrument of what is held to be more fundamental, such as the national destiny, or the folk soul, or the workers' revolution, or the East's independence of the West.

There seems to be some contradiction here, but it is only apparent. In our Western tradition the state has never in theory invaded the realms of culture, craft and religion; yet it is here in the West that hopes are placed upon the state for a recovery of community by all who do not believe in a recovery of predominantly economic bonds, whereas in the recent Eastern and Central European revolutions society overcame the state. In régimes which are openly totalitarian the state is captured by a political party which speaks in the name of some community programme. Trotsky cried: 'the state must be destroyed once more', and the original Nazi revolution in Germany was in a sense an outbreak of popular energies against the overweight of the German state. It should be noted, however, that Stalin, at the 16th and 18th Party Congresses of 1930 and 1939, announced that the party no longer holds that the state will wither away before the victory of classless socialism in all countries. Such a heresy against Marxist orthodoxy made sur-

The Political Faiths

prisingly little stir; it was got over by one of the most skilful turns of dialectic argument. When state power is invested with cultural and moral and social monopoly it is more dangerous to the division of powers and plurality of functions than plain state domination, for a society which is so fully conditioned that all its organs work uncritically for the fulfilment of one of its communal aims has no principle in it by which the trend can be challenged. Society is supreme and the state marches in its clothing. So the political faiths of our day are really social faiths using the vast apparatus of state power.

I am asserting that the state principle is no more able to constitute the bonds that make a society than the market principle. Although these two have been rivals of a sort during the last two centuries, we can say a little more precisely how the predominance of market relations under capitalism made inevitable the rise of the political faiths of our time. Three reasons seem to stand out to account for modern communities resorting to the state as the instrument of social restoration. Something was needed to counteract the dislocations of a market economy ceasing to function, or functioning only at the cost of arousing a widespread sense of injustice and bewilderment. Then, a social reality was needed which would give status and a sense of significant function to the mass of men, both of which had been alienated from them by the industrial and commercial system capitalism had created. And, in the third place, an object of reverence, a repository of the social good, had to be found which would engage men's religious and emotional attachment in the void left by the disappearance of a specifically 'sacred' sphere of life, and in the cold relations of contract, bargaining and mechanization which had replaced the warmth of pre-economic unities. Whatever conclusions we may come to about the success or failure of the state principle in meeting these needs, the firm belief that it would, or the dim sense that after all nothing else offered on a big and deep enough scale, or just the blind seeking for something lost—these amply account for the growth of faith in the state principle as the power for re-forming society.

On the first of these reasons there has been a growing volume of radical criticism of capitalist economy on grounds of its eventual unworkability, due to some contradictions in its structure and to

The Political Faiths

the sense of resentment it breeds. From the approaches to state socialism in the later utilitarians, through the many ramifications of Karl Marx's analyses, the doctrines of the Fabians and syndicalists, to the fascist, communist and national socialist revolutions we can trace a variegated opposition to the market economy of capitalism. Some of these movements definitely looked to the state as the organ of a more stable and just economy, and others, while critical of this solution, recognized its oncoming sweep with resignation or dismay. Apart, however, from the more familiar causes of resort to the state as the supreme economic organ for co-ordinating or administering the economic affairs of the community, there are one or two considerations of special importance for our examination of the situation. One is that moves towards political direction of economic life are not entirely a tendency counteracting the market economy. In some respects it is the fulfilment of the trends in that economy. With the growth of trades unions on the one hand, and of vast industrial and commercial management corporations, state control is on the way whether it be by extending an existing process or by a concern that any dangers of social irresponsibility in such great power groups must not be allowed to develop. And, less consciously, 'the rational organization of industrial production became one of the strongest impulses towards a democratic reorganization of the political order and of the educational system, and thus of the modern national state. . . . A neo-feudal attitude of protectionism is spreading and is using the organizatory forms of the new social and political order for restricting competition. . . . Already the final phase of the self-annihilation of industrial dynamics comes in sight: subjection of economic autonomy and free exchange to political regulation and centralized planning.'[4] A second factor is the need for some authority to stand over the potential struggle between Owner Management and Labour Unions, a struggle which in England becomes more tense as its economy becomes less able to recover the relative peace between capital and labour achieved, as for instance between 1850 and 1882, when they could jointly and freely exploit the pre-capitalist world. Moreover, state allocation and rationing of material, labour and land and technical competence may well

The Political Faiths

become nearly absolute owing to this technical civilization, in both its capitalist and socialist forms, failing to provide for its own reproduction. Industrialism has relied upon the social capital stored up in its own and then in foreign pre-capitalist communities; it has used that nearly up, created a world where its costs rise steeply and where native peoples themselves enter the industrial and market field. Capitalism could deliver goods cheaply so long as it did not have to meet this cost of reproducing the basis of society, and labour shared the profits. As Rosenstock-Huessy puts it: 'The modern employer comes into a settled community like a bull into a china shop. He lives by murdering the pre-capitalist orders. But he and his own labour forces still receive all the moral order they have, from the values of this same pre-capitalist world which capitalism underbids.'[5] The shrinkage of the world as a cheap source of supply and an open sink for manufactures is presenting the older industrial societies with the task of reproducing those of its basic assets that in theory could be created again—such as its animal and vegetable supply, its community impulse, its moral and spiritual order, its neighbourhood and craft loyalties; and the task of husbanding its irreplaceable assets like its open spaces, its water-supply, its mineral wealth. And at the same time these industrial societies have to turn out a stream of secondary products and services which their populations have been led to want. Capitalism stimulated appetites which looked like being met in its lucky day and which the ensuing socialism still counts on satisfying. The job of allocating natural resources and energies between the two demands of reproduction and current satisfactions is one which no recent political system has dared to take seriously. But the cumulative emergencies arising from the dissipation of basic sources of economic life drive still further towards state ownership or control over community assets.

Again, disappointment at not getting what industrialism promised breeds resentment and a demand for more equal distribution of a diminishing revenue. The assumption, which was valid in the period of expansion, that deprivation here generally meant that some had too much there, continues to operate. And what but the state will be trusted to do the equalizing? Further, a

The Political Faiths

special case arises for societies which set up full employment as an economic goal. Such a society to-day has to attempt two incompatible things: to keep people busy where they are, whether their work is reproductive or extravagant of basic assets, and to get people from secondary to primary occupations as this becomes more and more urgent. No sectional interest can dare to handle this tricky and distasteful dilemma and the population itself has not the awareness or the will to cope with its seriousness. These are but a few of the reasons for increasing *dirigisme* of economic life on the part of the state, over and above the reasons stated by the great socialist propaganda movements. They tell why every modern government acts as an 'abnormal' government, taking greater powers to deal with one emergency after another. The state principle grows in influence as the market economy ceases to function.

The second reason we are considering for this growth is that citizenship in the political sense has come to acquire a kind of substitute value for the sense of status and functional significance in occupation, both of which were steadily weakened by the economic enterprise of capitalism. The economic benefits of that enterprise could not be a sufficient substitute for emotional attachment to a social order to which men felt they belonged, however ground down they might be, and where they could see with their eyes that their labour or exploits were purposive and contributory. The long-range blessings of industrialism are too much things to be inferred rather than seen, so that a convinced loyalty to it is confined to the few who can take long views. No wonder that the majority think of those long-range benefits as only the interests of a minority. Schumpeter writes: 'There are the daily troubles and expectations of trouble everyone has to struggle with in any social system—the frictions and disappointments, the greater and smaller unpleasant events that hurt, annoy and thwart. I suppose that every one of us is more or less in the habit of attributing them wholly to that part of reality which lies without his skin, and *emotional* attachment to the social order—i.e. the very thing capitalism is constitutionally unable to produce—is necessary in order to overcome the hostile impulse by which we react to them. If there is no emotional attachment, then that impulse has its way

The Political Faiths

and grows into a permanent constituent of our psychic set-up.'[6]

Now, the state can never be an object of emotional attachment which could replace a man's roots in home, property, neighbourhood and craft association. But when these ties have been weakened by the proletarian condition of workers, then the fact of citizenship in the national state is more and more turned to as the sole guarantee of status and the sole provider of purpose. This is not altered by the fact that the causes of disaffection are then projected upon governments instead of upon the propertied and managerial classes. In fact, as society becomes less pluralist and more unitary under state direction, all social resentments become directed against the state, and the state tends to redirect them against foreign powers. State socialist régimes are clearly less international than earlier ones with a more mixed internal grouping of classes and powers. But resentment against the state in advanced collectivist societies is one side of the expectation that as citizens men can find somewhere a reality which treats them for what they are and not only for what they can do and deserve. And where state collectivism has not arrived the faith is all the stronger that there perhaps man can recover a sense of status. And as to function, under capitalist industrialism, with its growing dependence upon unskilled operations, with the subdivision of labour, with its call upon standardized repetitive productive actions, with its mammoth corporations, a man's work becomes far removed from something he can think of as being done for its own sake or as contributing to the well-being of his family, his fellows or his locality. To my knowledge there has not, since the birth of the capitalist epoch, ever been a 'quality strike', or a withdrawal of labour in protest at having to do bad or shoddy work. It is with this vocational emptiness that there comes at least the theoretical prescription that by working for the state the artisan is serving the needs of the community as a whole. It is pretty thin as a concrete incentive, but for want of anything more living it has a moral and propaganda force. Two recent authorities who are not themselves upholders of collectivism have seen the lack of status and of a sense of function, as at the root of much unrest and resentment, where even the victims suppose that it is due to purely economic discontents. Peter Drucker, having shown that not only the unemployed man, but also the automatic mechanized unskilled worker who is the more efficient for not understanding the whole process, suffers from a lack of function and status, though he may consciously have come to value only income and economic wealth. He goes on to say: 'What the people really demanded during the last decade was not only economic security but social status and function. . . . Economic security as a political programme ignores the most important lessons of the last twenty-five years; that economic satisfactions are only negatively effective in society and politics. The absence of economic satisfactions creates severe social and political dislocations. But their presence does not by itself constitute a functioning society.'[7] And Professor Röpke reminds us of the alarm felt by Le Play in France, and Jefferson in America, at the prospect of the peasants and workers becoming changed into a propertyless and nomadic proletariat on the one hand, and a capitalist plutocracy on the other. He then defines proletarianization as a 'highly dangerous sociological and anthropological state which is characterized by lack of property, lack of reserves of every kind (including the ties of family and neighbourhood), by economic servitude, uprooting, massed living quarters, militarization of work, by estrangement from nature and by the mechanization of productive activity; in short, by a general devitalization and loss of personality.'[8] And again: 'Congestion, regimentation, proletarianization, collectivization and the disappearance of the little properties of the masses, who incidentally are being continually recruited afresh from the crumbling middle classes, all these are discharged like a river into a mass delta, ordered, led and always further financed by the state, and in conjunction with the state together with its apparatus for taxation and social services, produce a society which is drying up individuality in favour of collectivism . . . the wider the span of proletarianization, the wilder become the cravings of the uprooted to be guaranteed social services and economic security by the state . . . (and) the greater part of the national income (is) claimed for and directed by the state.'[9]

These quotations depict the movements which meet together in erecting the political state into the sole organ for giving the mass of men the psychic and physical standing in society which capitalism could only succeed by cutting away. I should repeat that it is *faith* in the state that is here emphasized as a social force, not necessarily appreciation of the result achieved. Of these results a modicum of economic security can and has been achieved, as in Britain, and it can last as long as the total economy survives. But the sense of having status and performing a significant function is something which no modern social system has conferred on the proletarian masses, except by some kind of non-economic totalitarian impulse. Hitler largely succeeded because he offered these satisfactions in a cause outside the economic sphere where it had quite broken down. The USSR does it by attaching to state power all the existing community feeling which a pre-capitalist society still possesses. But with rapid industrialization this community feeling has to be fortified or replaced by the stimulus of nationalist sentiment, of conviction that it is the morally superior industrial society crusading in an otherwise doomed world, and of the kick it gets from challenging the older industrial powers.

In the third place, political faiths replace economic ones because at this stage in the decline of capitalism the state tends to take on a sacred character, or becomes the central council of a society on which is projected the ineradicable need for a realm of 'the holy'. This increases with the disappearance of dynastic and monarchic rulers with their semi-sacred attributes. Hitler was the legatee of the European dynasties which Woodrow Wilson abolished; Lenin and his successor inherit the mystical reverence accorded to the Tsars. In England men insist on maintaining the kingship as a rallying point of social and personal loyalties which cannot find an outlet in the impersonality and anonymity of the economic and civic structure. So here the only feeble symptom of any tendency to identify the political with the sacred realm is the Labour Party's habit of talking like a prayer meeting.

It is one of the strange features of the twentieth century that the state is tending to be given the value once attached to the church. This is due to the weakening of a religious and intellectual culture which could stand a separation of political and religious authority

The Political Faiths

so long as both were understood as having a common underlying warrant and a common allegiance to the religious and moral axioms of Christendom. This separation was a large factor in creating a framework for liberty and enterprise. In one respect the relegation of the state to a secular or civic role, as distinguished from its being a divine object of veneration, begins with the Old Testament theocracy. In Mesopotamia 'political influence was wielded in the universe only by those members who, by virtue of the power inherent in them, could be classed as Gods'; in Egypt the divinity was the God-King; Alexander introduced the ruler-divinity to the Hellenic world and it then passed into the Roman orbit. In contrast to all this the Hebrews originated the conception of a social order established by God, but having no sacred or absolute character of its own. Holiness and absolute sovereignty belong to God alone who transcends every cosmic reality and every human institution.[10] The Old Testament never confounded the kings with the priests, though the former were always the Lord's anointed. The Christian Church still further dissociated the civil from the religious power by its supernatural and trans-local structure. This separation was affirmed by Christ's distinction between the things that belong to Caesar and those that belong to God, and Christendom has largely been the history of tension between the princely and the sacerdotal functions, the two powers having sometimes been taken as symbolized in the 'two swords' of Luke xxii, 38.[11] But while the Hebrew-Christian tradition de-divinized the state, it held the political as well as the priestly order to be under God, although in a distinct mode. Rulers were considered responsible for bringing acts of state before the judgement of righteousness understood as the holy will of God. With the rise of the modern national state this link with the sacred order was for all practical purposes completely broken and the 'secularized' state, in the full contemporary sense of the term, appeared. Since then not only the state but also society and its culture have become secularized, and the economic age has strengthened the place of raturalist elements in secularism by making them subserve the awakened race for wealth and influence backed by economic power. Capitalism gave to the perennial self-

The Political Faiths

interest of man and his grabbing propensities the weapon of rational calculation; and socialism seeks to add to the rational handling of means for economic ends the rational planning of the economy as a whole which has seemed so absent in the capitalist epoch. And, as Engels was never tired of repeating, the increased sense of man's power to master his environment led to his emancipation from any allegiance to a sacred realm. This is true, but only at one human level. On another level in the human being the need for a 'holy community' creeps in and demands satisfaction. As early as the French Revolution the new secular state was panoplied in the armour of a churchly society.[12] Later the praises of a goddess of Nature and her adorable daughters, Virtue, Reason and Truth, were sung by Holbach to invigorate the static world of Newtonian physics. To-day it is society itself that takes on the lineaments of a divine absolute, with the state corresponding to the first Person of the secular divinity. In one sense it is the end of the lay state of the last three centuries; in another it is a reaction in the depths of man's being against the utilitarian and contractual character of nineteenth-century bourgeois society—a blind heave of the modern soul to find a substitute for the lost religious foundations of life and a lost spiritual community. 'No one can understand the German's exaltation of the "State" unless he knows that it is rooted in the depreciation of a visible church.'[13] The *mystique* of the state will grow with the dominance of life by mechanization and economic motives. This whole trend is an aspect of the curious way in which the twentieth century is reversing the whole course of Western history. That history began with the disentangling of the sacred and the civic realms. Because the modern epoch in which capitalist liberal rationality played such a decisive part arose with and then accentuated the 'secularization' of life, the twentieth-century political faiths are reverting to the identification of the two orders.

What happened in Italy and Germany, what is still going on in USSR and Eastern Europe and Asia came by revolution; in the West it happens by drift and by *ad hoc* dealing with one emergency after another. We do not know whether this difference between the West on the one hand and Eastern Europe and Asia on the other will remain mainly a difference of method and tempo only, while going in the same direction; or whether two quite different kinds of community will emerge. It is quite clear, however, that the moving impulse is different. Faith in the state in the West is the result of inability to see any other counterweight to the freely operating market principle. Considerable light has been thrown upon the transformation of our time in respect of this distinction between society and state and their fusion to-day, by Mr. Christopher Dawson in his book *Beyond Politics*. Here are a few relevant passages. 'While English thinkers, whether Liberal or Conservative, recognized that society transcends the State, they did not realize the need for any deliberate organization of the more political social functions. They believed that these things could be safely left to nature and to the free activity of individuals or, alternatively, to nature and social tradition.'[14] Mr. Dawson makes the point that the relatively modest place the state has had in liberal societies, where one power was checked by many others, was due to society having a fairly common culture and set of values, and as we have emphasized, these were mistaken for the permanent apparatus of human existence. When they begin to be dissipated the two independent orders of secular culture and 'the vast system of financial commercial and industrial relations which we know as the capitalist order, become centrifugal and disintegrating forces' —though they had vastly increased men's natural and spiritual resources. 'This first became plainly evident', says Dawson, 'in regard to economics, and it was here that the first conscious attempt was made to restore unity of direction and bring the economic order under the control of the community. This was the origin of Socialism and in a sense of all the totalitarian movements, for the attempt to unify the political and economic orders led almost inevitably to the confusion of social categories and the attempt to extend state control to every sphere of social life.'[15]

To that understanding there has to be added that Soviet communism has an entirely different origin. There society had not been through the liberal experience. A much more tribal or clannish organization with a sacred value attached to society itself has begun to take over the powerful social mechanics of the West—its

The Political Faiths

state apparatus, its economic and industrial outlooks, and its technical frenzies—and harnessed all these to a pre-capitalistic group solidarity. It is a very tough combination and has the same kind of *élan* which possessed Western industrialism in its early stage before it made too many inroads into its pre-economic foundations. In Mr. Fitzroy Maclean's *Eastern Approaches* you will read that what the peasant tribesman near the Afghanistan border regards his citizenship of USSR to mean is that it has introduced to him the motor car, the wireless, cheap scent and flimsy clothing, things which Western capitalism could offer pretty well.[16]

But the decline of capitalism is a Western phenomenon as was its rise. In this region the elevation of the state principle to counteract the free play of market forces and to give cultural forces a direction which was lost by breach with tradition, is to be seen as a heave of the Western soul away from one tragic eccentricity. As we should expect from our previous analysis, the state assuming this function becomes itself a new form of eccentricity, for the state in the West has never been more than an organ of society; it could not be its creator or sustaining principle. And the state is not really the counterweight to the unstable unities made by exaggerated economic relations. The state in its modern form builds upon man as citizen, and as it grows in power it tends to squeeze out or submerge all other human relationships. Neville Figgis, in his important work *The Churches and the Modern State*, said that 'What we actually see in the world is not on the one hand the State, and on the other a mass of unrelated individuals, but a vast complex of gathered unions, in which alone we find individuals, families, clubs, trade unions, colleges, professions and so forth.'[17]

For the origins of the state principle we must go to another authority, Edward Jenks, who explains in *Law and Politics in the Middle Ages* how the disentangling of the individual from the clan is one side of the same process that makes the state supersede the clan. The state is not the enlargement of the clan; there is no identity of principle between the two; the success of the state means the destruction of the clan. 'The clan is a community of groups, the state is a community of individuals.'[18] Jenks held, I think correctly, that there was and is an implacable struggle between them. He also held that 'In the long run the state is victorious all along the line.'[19] That has not seemed so certain since he wrote these things half a century ago, and he himself suggests why it may not be so though he did not draw this conclusion. 'No doubt', he wrote, 'as far as efficiency pure and simple is concerned the principles of the state are sounder than the principles of the clan . . . but gentile (i.e. clannish) ideas spring from instincts deep rooted in humanity and they cannot be entirely neglected. . . . While gentile ideas do not make for efficiency, at least they make for stability.'[20]

This brings out what I want to emphasize. Both the state principle with man treated as bare citizen, and the market principle with man treated as bare economic unit (I am abstracting from a tendency; fortunately men in the concrete are never so silly as their theories), both these represent very advanced constructions of the human spirit and intellect, built on to the substance of society made up from clan, associative, geographical, and religious groupings. They are artificial in the strict sense of the word, and we need not fall into the romantic error of concluding therefore that they are bad. But we have to make two generalizations: one, that neither is the principle of social healing; that must take place on a sub-economic and sub-political level. Two, that when the state principle is invoked as a remedy for the sickness of a society overweighted by market and contract relationships, then the real disorder is more effectively concealed.

I cannot add to the vast literature of twentieth-century political movements or analyse the revolutionary character of those which seek to keep the breakdown of the world economic and trading system outside their own borders. But we can see how it looks in terms of the religious account I have sketched. Recourse to the state principle is one of the swings of the modern collective soul pulled by man's essentially associative nature. Of course, this is made into practical programmes, into political theories, into moral, economic, cultural, or national aims. Because man is a spirit-centred creature he mostly likes to clothe the tug of his nature in the panoply of a deliberate purpose. The state principle, even when it is merely the instrument of one communal urge seek-

The Political Faiths

ing to subdue all others, always misses the fulfilment of man's associative nature. At least it does so when invoked as the restorer of damaged community relations. This is the outstanding example in our time of the process we outlined earlier. It is a response to man's urge for centrality away from one false position. If the state principle is taken as the essence of human togetherness instead of its product under certain specialized conditions, it becomes itself a deforming principle.

Tendencies in the direction of fusing all social and cultural activities into state activities—and giving the fusion the form of a great church, for that is what it amounts to—follow inevitably from the efforts to recover balance within the one-dimensional temporal plane. The balance is upset the other way. I will enlarge on this a little.

For one thing, we may recall that, as primitive, natural, clan or tribal organization gave place to the earlier civic and agrarian structures, natural, blood and neighbourhood tie could no longer be the only cohesive power; so there had to be ethics, legislation, professional custom and so on, something more deliberate and structural than Nature itself equipped men with. Precepts, constitutions, covenants, rules and codes appear as the way in which the social essence of man works to overcome the factors of egoism and dissociation, which get a longer run when relations are more impersonal, civic and contractual than when they are tribal. This is a great step in the history of man. Some of you may know Denis Saurat's pointed illustration of this fact that precept comes in when Nature breaks down. He puts into the mouth of a French *curé* the saying: The good God gave us a commandment that children should love and honour their parents, for it is not natural for children to love their parents. He pronounced no commandment that parents should love their children; no commandment was needed, for it is natural. That is why parents and children do not understand one another.[21]

Now there is a limit to the extent to which law, ethics, contract and government can go. They serve and make possible richer and more enterprising kinds of society. But there must be a network of native communal bonds of various kinds at the basis of civic society. That is partly because the regulations and codes are never completely effective and human perversity distorts or gets round them; it is also because no society of people can live entirely on the level of conscious social conformity—they would soon be worn out if they tried. When therefore the more elemental texture of society is broken up, as it has been in a predominantly economic age, more and more demands are made upon men and groups for deliberate and witting behaviour for the good of the social whole. And when national and political and economic societies are very big and complex, these demands to serve the good of the whole get beyond the powers of even the best-intentioned to envisage or to carry out. Then the omnicompetent state rides in as the moral and cultural preceptor and takes the place of Church. That is what rightly worries Professor Hayek who wrote, in *The Road to Serfdom*: 'The state ceases to be a piece of utilitarian machinery intended to help individuals in the fullest development of their individual personality and becomes a "moral" institution—where "moral" is not used in contrast to "immoral" but describes an institution which imposes on its members its views on all moral questions. . . . In this sense the Nazi or any other collectivist state is "moral" while the Liberal state is not.'[22]

That is one reason why the state takes on a sacred character. I have referred to several others. I will re-state the one which seems to me the most far-reaching. The growth of over-riding economic and political relationships to the undoing of more natural interdependences has taken place along with a decline of religion and a loosening of men's hold upon the reality of God and a sacred eternal realm on the inner side of things. Religious faith gives men a sense that they have a status in the universe, whatever happens in the rough and tumble of history. They require the conviction of having status in their relation to reality as whole and in their immediate human setting. While we have been correctly taught that contract relations mark a great advance over relations based only on status, they cannot entirely supersede them. Some part of life must be established for men to be adaptive in others. The conclusion of this compressed argument is that as men have steadily lost the feeling of status in their community and at the same time in

The Political Faiths

the eternal realm, both social and religious status are sought for in the fact of citizenship. The growing omnicompetence of the state thrives on this status starvation in modern Western societies. And the need is the more easily filled by the state when people feel less and less significance in their work, less establishment in their homes and see their locality knocked out of recognition during half a lifetime in the cause of development.

The move towards giving the state and society a sacred character is of course more blatant on the Continent. In 1935 an authority could write: 'As the achievement of preliminary success receded into the background, Bolshevism itself entered a religious phase. Nowadays it has its god, its holy scriptures, its Church, its dogmas, its inquisitions, and its heretics.'[23] Mussolini said in one of his speeches: 'The Fascist state is a force, but a spiritual force which embodies in itself all forms of the moral and intellectual life of man ... it is the soul of the soul.'[24] Bergmann's *Twenty-Five Theses* began: 'I believe in the God of the Germanic Religion who works in Nature, in the sublime spirit of man.'[25] All this is old and familiar and we may think it irrelevant, but it is only the extreme and feverish form of an inevitable pressure to get in somewhere the Holy Community which men need. If it is not found in a church which transcends historic societies, its sacred quality is transferred to one of these. I have often quoted a revealing passage from the fourteenth of Fichte's addresses to the German Nation, in which he lets out the logic of this tendency.[26] He says that man is made for an eternal end and is not inwardly content with a more limited one. But he uses this truth to tell his compatriots that the individual person must therefore find his total purpose and significance in the life of his *volk*, for that, he averred, has eternal life. You see what an easy but fatal mistake this can be. The race lasts much longer than the individual on earth, but the race still belongs to the temporal order: and if you give it the supreme value of the eternal you subordinate the person merely to a larger wave of temporal succession. All totalitarian oppressions are of this nature. Man has an inalienable link with the eternal world, but when he objectifies its pull upon him and makes absolute something in his temporal existence, then in the end he must lose his freedom.

The Political Faiths

To return from these high themes, if we can see that the period of declining capitalism has the character I have suggested, it helps us a little to disentangle a confused controversy. We could name it after two recent participants and call it the Hayek-Finer debate. Professor Hayek wrote *The Road to Serfdom*, pointing out that tendencies which are undoing the liberal society, such as he had seen in Central Europe, he now saw coming with almost imperceptible relentlessness in Britain. He then proceeded to argue that the freedoms and loose associations and cultural vitalities which are threatened depended upon the autonomy of the economic function with its elements finding their own price in a free market, to use my own language. Then came a rejoinder entitled *Road to Reaction* by Dr. Finer, insisting that accumulations of monopolistic economic power and great inequalities of wealth and advantage, made the coveted freedoms and opportunities impossible for the mass of people.[27] Therefore, the argument proceeded, the citizenship status afforded by the planning and welfare state was an instrument of those very freedoms and opportunities. I think this controversy is at cross purposes because both sides ignore the process I have been concerned to explain. The positive values which Hayek wants to preserve or recover were not created or sustained by the exchange and market system; they partly co-existed with it and survived until the pre-capitalist fabric into which they were woven had worn so thin that the economic pattern had no reliable basis. Then the state had to enter the social, moral and cultural field as the only possible cohesive. As a measure of cohesion it served clumsily, but as a curative power it cannot of itself be effective.

For the state to be true to its proper political function it must count on the same social health underneath as the market principle needed to achieve its transitory triumphs. To know how this health underneath is to come about may be beyond the insight of the present generation. But so long as the economic and the state principle monopolize the competition to be the constituent of social reality, their rivalry is bound to be a kind of war of the pseudo-religions. For when the final truth about man is sought in the immanent order, then one's own side is equated with the sacred and the other identified with the unholy. When society

The Political Faiths

seeks the source of unity and meaning anywhere short of the God who transcends as well as acts within the world, some human and historic position its put in the place of the displaced transcendent. Then there is bound to arise a campaign against religion which seems to the contestants to be either smugly above the battle or slily supporting the other side.

NOTES

1. Lionel Robbins, *The Nature and Significance of Economic Science* (London 1932), p. 15.
2. Aldous Huxley consistently makes it a count against the Hebrew-Christian view that it contradicts the tenet in which he equates the Fall with the Creation: 'The incomprehensible passage from the unmanifested One to the manifest multiplicity of nature, from eternity to time, is not merely the prelude and necessary condition of the Fall; to some extent it *is* the Fall.'—*The Perennial Philosophy* (London 1950), p. 209.
3. Genesis iii, 5.
4. A. Löwe, *Economics and Sociology* (London 1935), pp. 113–14. Löwe refers to similar considerations in Max Weber and Karl Mannheim. cf. B. de Jouvenel, *Problems of Socialist England* (London 1947), chap. 29, on the mammoth structures of modern economy.
5. E. Rosenstock-Huessy, *Out of Revolution* (New York 1938), pp. 88–9. On the working assets of modern man and his economy, see the dire warning given in Michael Roberts, *The Estate of Man* (London 1951).
6. J. A. Schumpeter, *Capitalism, Socialism and Democracy* (London 1943), p. 145.
7. Peter F. Drucker, *The Future of Industrial Man* (London 1943), chap. IV.
8. Wilhelm Röpke, *Civitas Humana* (London 1948), p. 140.
9. Ibid., p. 141.
10. For an account of Egyptian and Mesopotamian notions of the divine state and their contrast to Hebrew views, see *Before Philosophy*, by H. Frankfort and others (Pelican Books), from which the above quotation is taken.
11. The above is a pitiably shorthand summary of an enormous span of history. For a fuller treatment, see Luigi Sturzo, *l'Eglise et l'Etat* (Paris 1937), chap. I; C. Lattey, S.J., 'The New Testament and the Pagan Emperors', in *Church and State* (London 1936); and my essay, 'Religion and the State', in *Theology of Society* (London 1947).
12. For the religious character of the French Revolution, cf. A. de Tocqueville, *L'Ancien Régime et la Revolution*.
13. E. Rosenstock-Huessy, *Out of Revolution*, p. 393.
14. C. Dawson, *Beyond Politics* (London 1939), p. 26.
15. Ibid., p. 16.

16. F. Maclean, *Eastern Approaches* (London 1949), p. 126.
17. J. N. Figgis, *The Churches in the Modern State* (London 1914), p. 70.
18. Edward Jenks, *Law and Politics in the Middle Ages* (2nd ed., London 1913), p. 77.
19. Ibid., p. 310.
20. Ibid., p. 311.
21. Denis Saurat, *The End of Fear* (London 1938), p. 29.
22. F. A. von Hayek, *The Road to Serfdom* (London 1944).
23. Bruno Meier, 'Moral Sanctions and the Social Function of Religion,' essay in *Christianity and the Social Revolution* (London 1935), p. 410.
24. B. Mussolini, *La Dottrina del Fascismo*, Section 12.
25. E. Bergmann, *Twenty-Five Theses of the German Religion*.
26. J. G. Fichte, *Reden an die deutsche Nation* (1808), 14 Rede.
27. Herman Finer, *Road to Reaction* (London 1946).

CHAPTER V

The Criticism of Religion

★

Tremendous upheavals in the religious thought and dispositions of the Western mind accompanied the early stages of what we have called the Decline of Capitalism. The nineteenth century in these parts of the world was, we may say, the field of three main religious forces. There were first the traditional Christian Church outlooks, with profound variations, including the Catholic, the Calvinist and the Anglican doctrines and cultures. Each of these in their church doctrine and salvation theology had resources for a specifically defined attitude to the social process, but only certain groups within the churches made use of these resources.

Secondly, there was what may be called the religion of capitalism, a kind of mixture which may be dubbed mechanism plus morals. In the earlier phase, the doctrines of the Hidden Hand and the Community of Interests had projected providence and ethics right into the mechanism of the unregulated market relationship; then that phase had given place to a more judicious outlook in which belief and conduct were expected to counteract from outside the impersonal workings of the dissociated economic exchange-relationships. The Utilitarians were sufficiently alive to what was going on to allow a certain contradiction to arise in their body of doctrine; one side of this contradiction clung to the natural identity of interests and preserved a *laissez-faire* attitude; the other realized that such an identity had to be moulded out of a natural diversity of interests; this trend proceeded towards collectivism or the welfare state.

The Criticism of Religion

The third religious influence, which we must dwell on for a moment, had two opposed movements in it which nevertheless are at one in having no positive critical attitude to the secular order. One was the kind of passive, subjective pietism which in the name of individual salvation held aloof from the enigmas and dilemmas of the social order. This attitude had largely invaded the historic churches but was preserved alive mostly in some of the free churches. Strictly speaking, this was a position in which there could be no Christian judgement on the structure of society in the name of a natural order for man—no Christian doctrine of the secular—only Christian judgement of the conduct of men within their corner of the structure. The other, the opposite tendency, was the identification of the Christian spirit with what seemed best in the historic scene, blessing the highest aims of society itself. It often took and still takes the form of faith in the power of disinterested altruism spreading from men touched by grace to the vast impersonal relationships of classes, corporations and national groups. It is the application to the social sphere of the premises of religious liberalism. Sometimes this meant an identification of the Christian message with an organized movement of reform, exemplified in the saying: 'Christianity is the religion of which Socialism is the practice.'

This crude account of religious forces, at a period when the interaction of Church and world was dissolving into dissociation, is something not only to be observed. It could be deduced; it could not help but happen. If a phase of cultural history has proceeded under the sign of an incarnational religion, as Europe certainly has, and then the world-affirming and the world-transcending elements in that incarnational dogma fall apart, what have you? You will inevitably have on the one hand the world's own movements throwing up their proper immanentist faiths—perhaps at first with a dash of Deism for traditional appearances' sake; but this soon fades out. On the other hand you will have a renunciation of any direct theological word about the fate of man in his historic setting and a move towards a pure individualist and apocalyptic religion. But you will also have trends within the religious bodies virtually to drop the dialectic relation of man's temporal and eternal refer-

The Criticism of Religion

ences, and to become assimilated to the world's own immanentist assumptions; this first takes a liberal and then a collectivist form.

The great Churches who still hold on to the fruitful tension between the eternal and the worldly references, and who find their theological warrant in incarnational doctrine, have perhaps not come firmly to grips with the split in the modern soul, the split wherein each half of their own truth has acquired an independent and therefore a false or heretical existence. One major requirement of so coming to grips must be an assessment of the force of the attacks on the Christian religion which this situation has called out. There were of course many criticisms of religion which had no particular concern with the social dissociations accompanying the liberal age; a great number proceeded from ostensibly intellectual and moral motives without awareness that society itself had become a problem. And many forms of secularist philosophy have appeared, some of them openly in criticism of religious beliefs, others with little conscious opposition to them. It will be useful to classify the main types of secularism with an interpretation of it made from a Christian outlook. Such a sketch will establish that secularism has been as much a characteristic of the intellectual atmosphere in which capitalism triumphed as it has been of the movements opposing it.

The ancient paganisms, the Bible and the Christian Church all have this in common, that they hold the source of all things to be a divine reality which transcends the world as well as operating in it. The secularisms of to-day have this in common, that they hold the meaning of the world to lie within itself. So we may use the adjective 'secular', for all its ecclesiastical origin, to denote a collection of working philosophies, bearing in mind that the purely rationalist and materialist outlooks which marked the secularism of the last century are only a small part of the secularism of the contemporary world. By far the most influential secularist movements of to-day have psychologically religious overtones which distinguish them from rationalism or mechanistic materialism. They are none the less atheistic, and they get their religious overtones by giving some level of human existence the absolute or sacred quality which genuine religion accords only to God.

The Criticism of Religion

The older materialists endowed the atomic substratum of things with all the potentialities of intellectual and spiritual development. A later phase gave biological existence the central place, with crude matter as a kind of backwash, while 'life' pushed forward to give birth to the gods. Then appeared the claims of psychology with the human psyche as the key to the management of existence, human salvation being found by communion with the libido. These are respectively materialist, vitalist and psychological forms of secularism.

Next comes a group of outlooks which virtually deify some phase of the historic process. Nationalism has in some phases been a substitute religion; Marxist Communism gives absolute and universal value to one particular social programme; Fascism definitely made the folk-consciousness into the finger of God. Democracy in England and America has almost been given the status of the Commandments and the Gospel.

Probably the most widespread and popular form of secularism in this country is that blend of naturalism and rationalism which believes in the emergence of rational, moral and social incentives as the result of the passage of time and history. It has misapplied the biological doctrine of evolution to society, injected into this conception the ethical and social aims of Western Europe while believing that those aims are incipiently part of Nature, whereas they are the products of a definite historic tradition. It then urges that the ethically good is to be defined by that which furthers the evolutionary process. Not all the intellectual and social revolts against this view in the history of the last half-century have shaken the naïve fideism of its champions in this country. We may call it evolutionary progressivism.

Lastly, the most seductive form of secularism, which can deceive the very elect, is that which interprets this evolutionary immanentism as the self-revelation of spirit, as in the massive idealistic philosophy of Hegel and his dependents. This has not much direct influence now, but it has two indirect descendants. One is the dialectical aspect of Marxism, in which the force of the Hegelian self-developing idea is transferred to the material and social struggle. And there is, secondly, the still surviving hangover in

The Criticism of Religion

religious circles of the Hegelian philosophy of religion, which passed for theology in a good many teachers of the past two generations (cf. Prof. J. M. Creed's examination in *The Divinity of Christ* Cambridge 1938, especially ch. III, 'Progress and Incarnation', and ch. V). Quite a serious cause of misunderstanding in religious thought to-day between two generations is due to the differing contexts in which is set the content of the Christian revelation, by the theological representatives of philosophic idealism, on the one hand, and by those who now feel the incompatibility of this idealism with the theology of the Bible, the Fathers and the liturgical tradition, on the other.

The main point about which clarity is necessary is that the essential characteristic of secularism is independent of the nature which secularism gives to what it regards as ultimately real; it is still secularist even when that reality is mental or spiritual, and not only when it is material or biological. All these outlooks stand over against the doctrine of God who is above and behind His creation and who meets it by covenanted and uncovenanted grace in His transcendent mode, as well as being operative in it by His immanence. It is the 'monistic' one-story universe of all forms of secularism which constitutes their common lineage. What Ranke said of Hegel, that in his philosophy 'Mankind is the growing god who procreates himself through a spiritual process immanent in his own nature' can be made to apply to any secularist doctrine by changing the adjective 'spiritual' to another appropriate one.

Now, any doctrine of man which dispenses with his relation to the Eternal God and with his need of a Saviour, fails to do justice to the double element in the human being which is the foundation of the Christian doctrine, namely his freedom and his creatureliness. Secularist views cannot find a point of unity behind this human duality. Therefore, in practice if not always in intention, they in effect deny the reality of one or other of these two facts.

We have, therefore, first, a group of interpretations that discount man's spirit-centred nature with its derivatives in his power of independent and disinterested thought, of moral responsibility, of historic and social decision. The various forms of naturalism

The Criticism of Religion

come under this head, in which man is nothing but a product of the process of Nature, though sometimes he is regarded as its high-water mark. There are the theories which regard him as merely the result of historic and social developments, as e.g. in the economic interpretation of history, or as solely an item in the political struggle. Determinism has also its psychological form, as in the view that thought and moral norms and character are all functions of primal urges that have been repressed, or, more crudely, that moral defect is a physiological abnormality.

And, lastly, under this head of deterministic views, though mixed with a voluntaristic principle, is a wholesale revolt against the complications due to man's intellectual and spiritual faculties, a revolt which preaches a recession to the stream of Nature. Chesterton parodied it: 'I wish I were a jelly-fish that couldn't fall downstairs.'

All these doctrines do insist upon what the Christian recognizes as man's creatureliness. He is a finite part of Nature, of history and of his terrestrial setting, and these outlooks crop up largely in reaction to the unreality and pretensions and frustrations of the opposite interpretations which exaggerate the power of man's rational, moral and creative faculties to bring his life to fulfilment. The plausibility of naturalist doctrines should remind Christians that man's fulfilment does not come by acts of decision or thought but by his life being redeemed at these indeliberate levels.

It is perhaps this other class of secularist theories which holds the dominant position in the working faith of the modern West. Here we have to do with a belief that the activities of the human spirit—man's thought, his will, his ethics, his techniques, his spirituality—can take complete control and overcome in their own power both the forces of evil and the limitations which belong to man in his earthly, historic and social existence. All these forms of 'spiritual secularism' assume that the root of evil and non-fulfilment lies in man's finitude, whereas in fact it lies in his disobedience to the laws of his being as set by the Creator. Rationalism, for instance, holds that the reason is completely above the conflicts, bias and relative outlooks that mark the rest of human existence, and can bring them to order, whereas the reason largely operates

The Criticism of Religion

within their limitations without being aware that it is so conditioned. Moral idealism assumes that good aims carry their own power, whereas they need sustaining by dogmas, by a culture that bends the soul in a certain direction, by the trend of the social environment, by institutions, and often by force. Another variant proclaims that all human organization and technical adjuncts are morally neutral, providing merely power to do good or evil, as if the will of man were entirely above and not conditioned by the apparatus he uses. Again, it is widely held that harmful conflicts of power and interest can be prevented just by the introduction of a strong moral motive, whereas the moral frailty of man demands a certain balance of power in society so that egoisms are curbed.

Further, the tendency to give final value to one's own way of life as a nation, or a class, or a civilization, as if it had transcended, in essence at least, all the one-sided and imperfect achievements of the past or of other modes of living—this is putting one particular construction of the human spirit in the place of the Kingdom of God. A good deal of planning, especially on a world scale, is preached in the hope that contradictions found on a smaller scale can be overcome by enlarging their area of operation, whereas this usually leads only to a change in the nature of the conflicts. And when education is advocated as the cure for the disintegration of a society or a culture, as if it could lead it from outside when in fact it is the child of the culture or society concerned, we are faced with a very exaggerated view of the freedom of the spirit over the less deliberate factors in existence, which are more matters of growth than indoctrination.

Besides these two classes of secular doctrines about man, each of which denies in practice one aspect of his double nature, there is a curious and ominous combination of the two. It is the working assumption of tendencies that make for loss of liberty. It consists in believing that the mass of men are entirely determined beings, but that a certain *élite*, with powers to plan, to control, to adjust psychologically the lives of the majority, are fully possessed of freedom and truth in deciding the good of the many.

The Christian understanding of man recognizes that these twin

The Criticism of Religion

forms of secularism arise out of a dissociation between two real aspects of human existence. There is a kind of pull-and-push rivalry between them. Human thought and history swing from the perversions of the one to the exaggerations of the other. There is no way out of this endless see-saw, except by recognition that behind the temporal order of human life there is the Divine Reality, and that submission to God and continued relearning of His laws, is the sole condition of man finding a unity of his freedom and his dependence.

We have paid some attention in these lectures to three dominant events which have come with the great reversal of the free-market economy and with the displacement of liberal outlooks by more consciously collectivist ones. Those three events have all been expressions of the attempt of the modern mind to work out on the one-dimensional plane of world process only, the full dialectic of human existence between its immanent and transcendent aspects. First, society itself, in mortal danger of disintegration by extreme dissociations, such as independence of economy from the rest of society, begins to take the place of the displaced transcendent and acquires absolute value; it gains a religious allegiance. Secondly, the political movements which in a more conscious way are pressing to overcome the dissociation, take on the character of religious faiths—and by reaction, the defenders of liberty also adopt a standpoint which puts the dispute far beyond the realm of political and economic controversy, into a realm where the conflict is between light and darkness. Thirdly, egoism and forces of evil fasten upon the positive positions in each side of the conflict—positive in the sense that they counter the other side's idolatry, and then men fight for their side with all the temper of religious fanaticism. This is inevitable so long as men see the terms of the dialectic which governs human existence as operating within the immanent order only.

A survey of the criticisms of religion brought up in connection with the sway and decline of capitalism seems to disclose seven main types. The first four need not detain us longer than is required for brief comment, relating them to the second three which are central to our theme. These four criticisms are, that religion

The Criticism of Religion

has been an instrument of oppression, that it directed human concern towards an eternal world to the neglect of this world, that its teaching of sinfulness diverted attention from defects in the social order, and that religion is an atavistic attitude due only to man's infantile inability, now being surmounted, to control his environment. In the first place, religion is criticized in socialist thought for being the deepest force for bourgeois reaction against the coming of a classless society. This criticism can be found in Marx's *Introduction to a Critique of Hegel's Philosophy of Law*, in Marx's and Engels' *German Ideology*, and in Dietzgen's sermons on *The Religion of Social Democracy*. It was summarized by Julius Hecker: 'Religion obscures the true earthly relations of men. It presents them in a perverted manner. It gives supernatural sanction to every form of exploitation and violence. It certifies existing institutions as part of an eternal, divine order. War, slavery, the factory system employing little children, poverty, even disease, have all been justified and sanctioned by religion. Lenin was perfectly right when he concluded that "all contemporary religions and Churches, all and every kind of religious organization, Marxism has always viewed as organs of bourgeois reaction, serving as a defence of exploitation and doping the working class".'[1]

Marx was not so crude; his attack is that religion served to offer a false consolation to the oppressed, and this led him to appropriate Charles Kingsley's phrase about opium for the people. As a stricture upon much religious opinion in the worst days of the Industrial Revolution the justice of this account must be admitted, but as a general statement it is false. In the period of the rise of capitalism both Catholic and Lutheran conservative influence was anti-capitalist; on the other hand Calvinism largely stimulated social change and could hardly be said to make for lethargy. Of course, it has to be recognized that fears of the disappearance of privilege and of economic dispossession are real enough, and when men suffer this fear, such religion as they have tends to sublimate their all-too-human emotions. But, more subtly, when socially revolutionary forces are attached to dogmatic presuppositions that overturn indispensable religious outlooks, then reaction proceed from deeper motives than concealed self-interest.

The Criticism of Religion

In the second place, religion was castigated for a real or alleged concentration upon men's other-worldly destiny, thereby making them callous or indifferent to the lot of man in his historic setting. It has been a widespread tenet that belief in an eternal world makes for servility, excuses injustice and deflects energy from worldly tasks. Lenin, for instance, wrote to Maxim Gorky: 'The idea of God has always numbed and dulled the social sense by substituting the dead for the living, being an idea of servitude.' One could say that an eviscerated version of Christian belief in another world beyond the temporal one—eviscerated so as to stress only 'the future life' and its compensations for the inequalities of this life, which some bad hymns with their beyond-the-bright-blue-sky motif have encouraged—give force to this criticism. Some other-worldly religiosity has been a refuge from responsibility in this world; but on the other hand belief in men's link with eternity has often stimulated their efforts on earth, by relieving them of the customary despair that follows from desperate concern about results. And doctrines of divine predestination have always encouraged rather than smothered an activist behaviour in worldly pursuits: 'It is an elementary syllogistic error to think that because the exploited classes find consolation in the belief in a future life, therefore the belief in a future life beyond the grave makes these classes incapable of struggle. The alternative for the exploited has not been belief *or* struggle, but belief *or* despair. There have been struggles in which both exploiters and exploited have had the same religious belief in a future life. . . . Belief in God has not prevented man from struggling against nature.'[2] Moreover, faith in a terrestrial fulfilment can be as much of an anodyne as a bad kind of flight to the skies. When dreamers of total world peace despise lesser measures of international decency; or when reformers resent partial moves towards a little more humanity and justice which fall short of their total programme; when fanatics will have nothing to do with anything in between chaos and their undated millennium on earth; then sub-lunar faiths are, as much as bad religion, opiates for the people. In order to be effectual in this world it is not enough to disbelieve in the other.

In the third place, it is averred that Christian belief in the sinful-

The Criticism of Religion

ness of man attributes to an ineradicable fault in human nature what is the result of a false social structure, and that this belief makes a human utopia impossible. The second half of that stricture is correct, but the implication of social indifference drawn from the first is illegitimate. True, Christianity does not believe that a human utopia is possible in history. But only some attenuated forms of Christian religion have used the universal contradiction in man, known as sinfulness, to relieve them of any concern about the order of society. There has been much social criticism from churchmen based on the assumption of a less unjust régime—a closer reflection in society of the natural law of human life—possible without waiting for the perfection of the saints. And the moral frailty of man has led to many Christian pronouncements condemning social contexts in which man as he is cannot live ethically without exceptional heroism, for he is neither superman nor angel. Moreover, a full Christian realism holds that belief in an historic utopia nearly always leads to the toleration of remediable evils this side of utopia—and often to a fiendish glorying in them. It will not allow that a false move now can make for a true society in some indefinite future, for Christianity by referring every event to an eternity present now, as well as to the past and future, holds that every moment and event has its proper moral quality; it makes as it were its mark on the eternal slate in its own present. Therefore it warns equally against such false trails to utopia as 'toleration of injustice for the sake of pie in the sky when you die' or 'oppression to-day for the sake of plenty the day after to-morrow', or 'the servile state to-day for the sake of the glorious freedom of anarchist harmony in the days to come'.

In the fourth place, comes the communist theory that religion belongs only to the stage of development where world forces appear mysterious to men, and that it will disappear with human control over human destiny. We find, for instance, N. Bukharin, in the *A.B.C. of Communism*, saying that: 'Throughout the entire mechanism of social production, there will be no longer anything mysterious, or unexpected . . . the mere fact of the organization and strengthening of the communist system will deal religion an irrecoverable blow . . . the transition from the society which makes an

The Criticism of Religion

end of capitalism to the society which is completely free from all traces of class division and class struggle, will bring about the natural death of all religion and superstition.' In this argument Bukharin is repeating what had been said by Engels when he described religion as an attitude which goes with man so long as there are 'extraneous' forces outside him which control his life and which he is not able to master. In that stage both the terrestrial forces of nature and the social forces of history are reflected in a mentality which projects gods out of these overwhelming powers. Engels jibes at Dühring for wanting to stamp out religion, for, says Engels, when mankind has controlled its earthly and social environment religion dies its natural death. 'When therefore man no longer merely proposes, but also disposes—only then will the last extraneous force which is still reflected in religion vanish; and with it will also vanish the religious reflection itself, for the simple reason that then there will be nothing left to reflect.'[3] All this suggests the following reflection. If man's compulsory recognition of 'extraneous' forces is the condition of religion, then when the capitalist-socialist rape of the earth has been completed, with the dire obedience that stage will impose on the race, we may expect some very big gods indeed in the religion of the future!

Much of the criticism of religion here listed in terms of Marxist attacks on Christianity could be paralleled in the literature underlying the race mysticism of German National Socialism where the *Folk-life* was proclaimed as the exclusive object of loyalty, a loyalty which is weakened by the Christian conviction of the eternal world, of the contradiction of sin within man, and of the significance given to the person by his direct link with God. Ernst Bergmann cried: 'Who dares to pass by blindfold six centuries' history of the German spirit, and to impose upon us Germans, even to-day, the non-germanized Jewish God of creation who rewards and punishes.'[4]

Now, however, we have to attend to some really big and serious criticisms of Christian religion which have emerged in the period of declining capitalism, though they are not exclusively related to that prolonged event. The criticisms are that Christian belief with its cult has made a schism in existence—especially between man

The Criticism of Religion

and Nature; secondly, in contradiction to the first, that it has regarded Nature as a base from which man must work, instead of combating it with sufficient thoroughness; and in the third place that Christianity has helped mightily to destroy social reality by attaching great significance to particulars—personal and historical.

The first count against Christianity is that it divorced man from Nature. This count, as it is associated with opposition to capitalism, begins with Robert Owen, a man of integrity who criticized the capitalism out of which he got his living. In his *New View of Society* he asserts: 'All religious systems are in part inconsistent with the works of nature, that is with the facts which exist around us . . . and therefore must have contained some fundamental errors, and it is utterly impossible for man to become rational or enjoy the happiness he is capable of attaining, until those errors are exposed and annihilated.'[5]

It is, however, with the two great movements of communism and national socialism that we get this concern to overcome the schism attached to social movements on the largest scale. In the thought of Marx and Engels we find an interplay of two principles, that man (even what for religion is his spirit) is part of Nature, and that he is called to the conquest and mastery of Nature. 'At every step', wrote Engels in his *Dialectic of Nature*, 'we are reminded that we by no means rule over nature like a conqueror over a foreign people, like something standing outside nature . . . our mastery consists in the fact that we have the advantage over all other beings *of being able to know and correctly apply its laws*.' And 'the more this happens, the more will men not only feel, but also know, their unity with nature, and then the more impossible will become the senseless and anti-natural idea of a contradiction between mind and matter, man and nature, soul and body. . . .'[6]

Henrik Ibsen had caught the same eagerness for a new immanentist gnosis. In his play *Julian the Apostate* he proclaims the arrival of the Third Religion: 'The reconciliation between nature and spirit, the return to nature through spirit, that is the task for religion. The Third Kingdom shall come. The spirit of man shall take its inheritance once more.'

This kind of criticism has other features: Marx held that religion

The Criticism of Religion

was a mask which concealed and made tolerable man's alienation from his true self. In his earlier writings he used philosophical language and put it thus: since man's essence cannot be realized in his actual existence, it must find expression in an idea. That idea is religion; so man has a double existence—an actual or worldly life and an ideal or heavenly one. In his *Critique of Hegel* he puts it: 'The criticism of religion is the first condition of all criticism.... Once the holy image which represents the aberration of man from himself has been unmasked the task of philosophy is to demask the aberration... The demand that the people should give up illusions about its real conditions is the demand that it should give up the conditions which make illusions necessary.'[7] We know that Marx attributed the alienation of man from his essence to private property, especially as it produced a contradiction between what he called productive forces and productive relations, that is, between man's economic possibilities and the social system.

The point I am here bringing out is that this criticism is attached to a more general attack upon what is sensed to be a dualism in the older conceptions of human life—spirit and matter, the ideal and the actual, mind and Nature. There are two things I want to say about that. First of all, when the criticism is made that idealism introduces a false schism in man, Christian Theology is in agreement with that criticism, especially when idealist ways of thinking seem to assume an unrelieved opposition between ethics and Nature; or when philosophers, having dropped belief in God as Maker of Heaven and Earth, require God as a hypothesis in morals; or when other exponents take the view that society as part of Nature has its own non-moral laws but individuals can act by ideals not dictated by Nature. You see, when a philosophy dismisses the reality of the transcendent God who is the source of unity between Nature and spirit, that philosophy must regard the duality or tension between these two as a dualism—and when it then seeks to overcome the dualism it can only do it by making one side of the duality a form of the other. Hegel transformed all reality into spirit; Marx and others read all spiritual and moral facts into Nature, making a kind of philosophic animism. According to Christian teaching there is an ultimate unity in the fact of God,

The Criticism of Religion

who is the ground of the world's existence and also in a special sense of the human soul. But it will not allow that unity to be counterfeited by the more cheaply achieved unity of explaining Nature in terms of spirit, or spirit in terms of Nature.

The second thing I have to say is that this type of criticism directed against religious presuppositions is not confined to socialist critics of the capitalist order. It seems to have been part of a large wave of thought seeking to overcome the dissociations of recent centuries. The critics projected that dissociation right back into Christianity itself and the whole history of religion. You had men like Nietzsche dissolving ethics into power, but retaining will; and then a symptomatic figure like Ludwig Klages regarding even will and consciousness as the destroyers of life. You had Hitler talking about thinking with the blood; and one, Hans Prinzhorn, a disciple of Klages, declaring that 'all human progress must be measured and valued with measures whose origin is extra-human, biotic—cosmic—or, in religious terminology, divine'.[8] In other words, the divine is equated with the life force. And there was even something of this protest against logo-centric civilization in Goethe, who made Faust insist on correcting the words of St. John's Gospel: 'In the beginning was the Word'—and substituting: 'In the beginning was the Act.' Now, all this move towards bringing human existence under one sign only, that of Nature, is a very significant part of nineteenth-century and twentieth-century thought. At the moment I just want to call attention to the way it informed men of anti-democratic and anti-rationalist sentiments as well as adherents of Marxist socialism. Werner Sombart, who became an apologist for national socialism, looked upon both capitalism and socialism as twin offspring of an over-rationalized age from which the German people were to rescue the world.

At this point we might recall how the upholders of the trader-spirit themselves believed that they had found the secret of working along with Nature's own work. This may seem confusing enough; well, I'm going to add to that confusion in a moment. But, before that, let me call attention to a recent English exponent of the view that religion itself has introduced a schism in man. He is Mr. Lancelot Whyte, whose book *The Next Development in Man*[9]

The Criticism of Religion

is, in my view, the one serious criticism of religion to have appeared in England in the last twenty years. The discovery of the soul is for him the fall of man, and in his own words, 'religion in the European sense is the operation of an incomplete substitute for complete organic integration'. He calls for the development of what he calls 'unitary man' in whom the duality of self and Nature has been overcome. He salutes Nietzsche and Goethe and Marx for pressing in the same direction, but reckons that some of them do not succeed in overcoming the European dissociation. Of Marx Mr. Whyte says, his 'warring soul projects its own dualism into history and generates his tremendous gospel of conflict'. Yet it was through Marx that the European dissociated tradition 'suffered its first systematic attack'. On my own account I will point out that the place where Marx sought to establish his unitary principle was in the economic basis of life as part of Nature's own process—and this is exactly where the capitalist mentality sought and thought it had found it. Communism in practice assumes something outside economics, namely at present certain nationalist aims of the Slav peoples, and calls it an aspect of Nature's dialectic. Capitalism assumed the European spiritual tradition and regarded it as part of Nature's forward movement now reaching its fulfilment in the market economy.

And now, to add to the confusion as promised, here is a second kind of criticism of religion brought in in connection with the upheavals of the capitalist period. It is the exact opposite of the type we have just been considering. Many of the older radicals and democratic humanists took the view that the trouble lay in the fact that mankind had not yet sufficiently emancipated itself from Nature. There was an inherent conflict between the natural world with its unconcern for persons, mind or ethics, and the spirit of man. What we need, therefore, they argued, is the triumph of the human ethical and social spirit over the internecine warfare of the natural order. You have to have grown into adult life before 1914 to remember the large place this view took in the movements of humanist idealism, in England, in France, and in America. Thomas Henry Huxley was quite ready to face such an ultimate dualism. 'The cosmic process', he declared, 'has no sort of relation

The Criticism of Religion

to moral ends.' Human evolution would mean, in his outlook, not a continuation but a reversal of natural evolution. He was honest enough not to twist out of the situation as he saw it an ultimate common ground which would be necessary in order to regard the world as a universe. His agnosticism was one of the many great things about him. It would be tempting to examine the outlook of men like Walt Whitman and William Morris from this point of view; but that must be resisted. The criticism I am sketching, however, has very recently been put forward in a remarkable book too little known: *Nature, God and Man*,[10] by Mr. W. B. Honey, the authority on porcelain. Mr. Honey, in his advocacy of socialism, is as hard on science as he is on theology for appealing to a Nature which has some normative significance. Science, he holds, while rejecting the religious myth has made a dogma of the unity of the world, postulating a single type of law to which all existence is supposed to conform, and has thus been forced to seek the origin of brotherly love in some innate tendency of Nature itself. But things like co-operation are foreign to the natural process apart from man. 'Man will oppose nature—and this is called Socialism.' It is to be noted that Mr. Honey regards the competitive features of the capitalist economy as natural. Instead of allowing man's labour to be bought and sold like a commodity at a market price, leaving his welfare at the mercy of chance and competition, society, says Mr. Honey, has accepted, or begun to accept, the principle of the living wage. It remains now to make a full and general application to human society of the humane principles which should replace the natural law of conflict and competition. On the origin of brotherly love and co-operation, Mr. Honey has the refreshing candour to say: nothing can be affirmed—it is sufficient to recognize the fact of their existence.

There is a third type of criticism of religion I must trouble you with. I call attention to the great anti-Christian thinkers of the last century. Christian theologians would do well to assess their significance. I will take two representatives, Feuerbach and Comte, both in revolt against what they detected as the atomization of the modern age. Ludwig Feuerbach provides an example of how modern unbelief can become a kind of atheistic gnosis. It was he

The Criticism of Religion

who reversed the Biblical 'God made man in His own Image' and built his account upon the dictum: 'Man makes God in his own image.' The Christian alienation between man as created and man as fallen is replaced by an alienation between ideal and real. And the ideal for him is still in terms of the Christian virtues: wisdom, goodwill, justice, love. But man is estranged from his true self, and his true self is not the person, but the collective being of humanity. Here are his very words: 'The distinction between the human and the divine is nothing else than the distinction between the individual and humanity.' And again: 'So long as love is not elevated into the rank of substance, of being itself, there remains behind it a subject who, without love, is still something, a monster without sympathy.'[11] I mention Feuerbach not because he was a great figure, though he considerably influenced Karl Marx to turn upside down the idealistic dialectic of Hegel and to use the same immanentist logic for an historic and naturalist interpretation. I mention him because he is such a very modern religious man without belief in God and because he states so clearly the results of squeezing all the facts of the human problem into the one-dimensional realm of process—facts which Christian theology holds can only be done justice to by the link in distinction between God and the world.

Auguste Comte was even more radical in his criticism of Christianity and in deifying the process of society itself. Both he and Feuerbach saw something more clearly than many verbal indoctrinators of Christianity. Comte said: 'The great fault of theologism was to have attributed to personality an existence which, linking each one directly to an infinite power, isolated it deeply from Humanity.'[12] He calls his new faith the 'Religion of Humanity'. Now this apotheosis of the social process in history was an inevitable reaction to the individualism of the earlier modern period, which had sought to uphold the significance of the individual person on the same immanentist plane. We see the onward march of what is called by the ugly word 'sociocracy' in the phenomenon of totalitarianism. We do not so easily detect that the same one-story view of existence underlies the unconscious assumptions of the remnants of liberal democracy and a good deal of liberal religion

The Criticism of Religion

which tends to confine God's action to His immanent work in creation. The language of the Bible and theology may still be used, but it is used to give colour and drama to the assumption of God as the dynamo driving the cosmic machine.

It is no part of my intention to make debating points out of the contradictory character of the main criticisms of religion. I wish rather to see whether we cannot begin to restate the questions in view of these mutually inconsistent attitudes held sincerely and forcefully to deal with a real human problem. It is certainly an odd situation we have been looking at. On the one hand, vast theories have grown up in fault-finding with disharmonies which seem to reach an unusual height in the period of capitalist economics, and these disharmonies were attributed to a dissociation in man between his spirit and his involvement in Nature. But this criticism backed up irrational and racial superiority as well as rational and socialist equality. Then we saw how the older democratic radicals and their modern representatives clung to the older duality between spirit and Nature as the only basis for their reforming efforts. Also, that society itself was made into an absolute in men like Comte as well as in Marx. Comte had used this conception in a conservative direction and projected a non-churchly hierarchy and calendar of saints and religious worship as the framework of his scientific society. Feuerbach, Marx and Comte preached a 'sociocracy' which would mend the divorce between Nature and spirit in human life. Others have followed the same line, aware that this divorce had something to do with Western man's incapacity to foresee or control the great industrial forces of the nineteenth century and their neo-technical forms in the twentieth. Because society is the field of interplay between the two sets of facts comprehended under the terms 'spirit' and 'nature', when they fall too far apart society itself is regarded as the reconciling comprehensive principle. 'Spirit' here stands for the forces in man that move from within outward, his will, thought, decisions, his powers of control, planning and freedom, and his devotion to action and causes.[13] 'Nature' in man stands for the influences that bear in upon him and his own participation in the earth's life, influences that condition and limit the exercise of his spiritual forces.

The Criticism of Religion

They represent the constraining and determining elements in man and society with which he battles or to which he submits. We have seen that the criticisms of religion divide according to whether the attack is upon religion's alleged failure to do justice to spirit or nature in human existence, or to its mishandling of the relation between the two. These criticisms have increased in volume as society and its thought were themselves unable to cope with the paradoxical attitudes to man and Nature in which they found themselves involved. It is as if religion were blamed for not saving human society from society's own dissociation, and as if the dissociations were due to the religious heritage. It is true that the religious heritage did create that separation of spheres of life which had made Western civilization and that at the same time it prevented the separation from becoming an outright dualism.

The extreme dissociation of spirit and Nature in man is a product of modern thought in a period of declining religious influence, and the world's own attempt to overcome it gave rise to the paradoxical nineteenth-century attitude to man and Nature. We must look at this a little more clearly. In the conscious thought of the time, before the reactions at the end of the period, man, including his spirit, was regarded as immersed in the stream of Nature. That is one side of the paradox. The other is that while in his mind man was being told he was a product of Nature, his dispositions were being formed rather by the fact that he was then taking his greatest steps in subduing natural forces to his will, in applied science and in the industrial revolution.

Now, it is this unstable combination of two things, the belief that man is part of Nature and the fact that he has become a would-be tyrant of Nature, that has been disastrous. It led to the uncriticized assumption that whatever direction our civilization took was a direction of Nature herself. History was regarded as Nature's highest self, and the revolts against this crude naturalism in the name of humanity—the moral and social protests—these too were attributed to Nature. Then we got the idea of progress, a misapplication of biological evolution to man's social and moral history. The Victorians in England were so excited at what their scientific men taught about change as the underlying reality, and

The Criticism of Religion

they were so convinced of the finality of their moral, social and intellectual positions, that they read their aims into the process of change itself.

Another result of this too easy resolution of the paradox is the habit of refusing to believe that men can in fact defy Nature—the earth's and their own—to the point at which human existence is threatened. It ignores the extent to which spirit can do violence to Nature. It leads man to neglect the need for conscious obedience to Nature, for discipleship, as it were, in this sphere. I don't think that this is a highly materialistic age of ours; it is rather a period of over-confidence in man's knowledge, ability and intentions, which leads to a defiance of his limitations, and this defect I mainly attribute to the inheritance from last century when men were so impressed by man's participation in Nature that they thought this at any rate could not go wrong. The nineteenth-century contribution did not in its outcome take man away from dependence upon God and remind him of his dependence upon Nature; it emancipated him in his consciousness, from obedience both to God and Nature. Part of the trouble was that thinkers were learning a great deal about continuity in the physical world and so they imagined that continuity was the only kind of unity in things. They found it hard to recognize a unity between such things as Nature and the inner life of man—a unity of polar opposites in the same field—such as Christianity affirms by knowing God as the author of both Nature and the soul. The Victorians had perforce to bring them into continuity with one another, for apart from a religious interpretation of existence, with God as the source of unity, men will always have to choose between complete incoherence or the making continuous what reality, which is less tidy than the intellect, has made discrete.

The eighteenth century had, on the whole, turned with relief to the harmonies of Nature away from the chaos of history and the human heart, just as the later Romantics were to seek solace in Nature and in the past from the aridity and emptiness of a utilitarian age. But the scientific and philosophical Victorians were not satisfied to leave human affairs without sense or significance. In order to give them a meaning, that is to say to find a warrant for human aims in some more ultimate realm of reality, they tended to project human ideals into the natural process. For them it was the ascendance of the nineteenth-century middle classes that defined human ideals, and having read all this into Nature they said, as it were: 'Look what an intelligent and purposive thing Nature is!' You find that in the weaker sides of Macaulay and John Stuart Mill, both of them very great men. More critical spirits like Huxley, greater than his more consistent colleagues and descendants, could not find the key to human problems in subhuman nature, and having no religious source of meaning, they paved the way for the fatalism of Bertrand Russell with its wistful picture of 'Man's lofty thoughts ennobling his little day' finally extinguished by 'the trampling march of unconscious power', and also for the pessimism of Hardy and Housman in literature.

A lesser man often tells us more about an outlook than its greatest representatives, for he exposes its unsolved problems more naïvely. One such was Thomas Henry Buckle, who wrote a *History of Civilization*. Without knowing what he did he summed up the whole paradox. On the one hand man is a child and product of Nature and cannot be understood in any other way; but on the other man is also scientist, engineer and trader—the rational being who subdues Nature. Buckle found a meaning for the whole human enterprise purely in terms of the future superseding the past; what man is going to be is good, what he has been is bad. European man, he says, is the bearer of humanity's destiny, for 'the tendency has been, in Europe, to subordinate Nature to man; out of Europe to subordinate man to Nature . . . the great division therefore between European civilization and non-European civilization is the basis of the philosophy of history.'[14] The terrifying simplicity of this typical last-century view becomes even more alarming when we notice that Buckle also sincerely held that war would disappear because the trained armies' desire for war would be over-ridden by the more intelligent and numerous civilians, that the free market would overcome natural jealousies and that increased communication and transport would dissolve hatreds and prejudices. In the same vein Cobden and Herbert Spencer thought that industrial man would be pacific, whereas pastoral and agricultural man had been combative.

The Criticism of Religion

The history of our time has proved every one of these predictions to be wrong. But their significance, at this stage of the argument, is that they express so crudely the fragility of the nineteenth-century attempt to bring man and Nature into some kind of co-inherence, after the breakdown of the traditional Christian realism which held together, without coalescing them, the two truths that man is involved in Nature but yet is not entirely of it, for he lives and acts with a status and powers not given by it.

There are only two conclusions to be drawn from this whole situation. The first is that the move to unify the two halves of man—which had split apart in our way of thinking—is part of what in an earlier lecture I called the pull of man's essential being away from an aberration. Those moves do not tell politically or economically in a democratic or authoritarian direction. But all the men who sensed something decadent about the post-Renaissance world allied their criticisms and counter-programmes with this struggle of the soul of Western man to overcome the modern dissociations.

Capitalism, with its abstraction of the economic, and especially of the exchange relationship—in fact, by trying to make them central—represents one result of this dissociation. But critics of liberal democracy, and projectors of socialist programmes who likewise build on the centrality of economics, use the unitary urge to back up their strictures.

The second conclusion is this. There is a very great deal in the charge that Western man has suffered from extreme dissociations—mind and body, spirit and Nature, trade and society, ethics and power, and so on. But it is not due to the discovery of the self or soul or mind, over against the rest of reality. This discovery is part of Western man's very history. You have only to read a book like Waldo Frank's *America Hispana* to learn how the natives of South America were impressed by the enterprise, the devotion and also the ruthlessness of the Europeans. Somehow this power of man's spirit—with its activities of reason, will, ethical principle, of worship and devotion and domination—remained a disposition when the religious setting out of which it grew was dissolved. Then we may say it became a poison.

The Criticism of Religion

Shall we put it this way? There are two progressions in human history, and they are not two aspects of one and the same. The first is towards greater differentiation, analysis, and division of the flux of existence. Unless there is general conviction that this multifarious character of existence is significant as the work of a unifying reality behind and beyond it, the differentiation turns into opposition and conflict in which human consciousness divides into camps by giving separate existences and standpoints the value of the whole. Mankind has therefore to hop about to maintain any kind of equilibrium. This tendency to make differentiation and separateness into opposition and conflict for absolute values is progressive evil. It is the good on which it fastens, for the destruction of one false absolute is a good work. It is God's judgement. But to give the instrument of God's judgement unconditional value is the Devil's deftest stroke. *Diabolus simius Dei.*

But another progression is possible which alone can counter the danger of either destruction in a conflict of idolatrous claims or of servitude to the compulsion of events. This is growth in religious understanding which, from the unfolding of the ultimate mystery of existence given in revelation, sees all that is in the light of it. No thing or movement becomes identified with the purpose of God, but the truth revealed from beyond history enables man to see God's action in all of it. God becomes the meaning of the whole, with all its affinities and contradictions to the divine order and all the bonds and oppositions within itself. But God is discerned as the meaning of the whole only where He is known as more than the whole. Therefore there is a close connection between loss of belief in God as transcending the whole, and the dissociations and conflicts which seem so much part of the fate of our time. Without a truly religious insight, the modern mind has divided the 'substance' of life, and now it does not know how to remedy that except by confounding the 'persons'.

The Criticism of Religion

NOTES

1. J. F. Hecker, *Moscow Dialogues* (London 1933), p. 201.
2. Tiran Nersoyan, *A Christian Approach to Communism* (London 1942), p. 40. cf. P. T. Forsyth, *This Life and the Next*, The Effect on this Life of Faith in Another (London 1918).
3. Frederick Engels, *Herr Eugen Dühring's Revolution in Science* (Anti-Dühring), Eng. tr. (London 1934, and later), p. 348.
4. Ernst Bergmann, *Deutsche Nationale Kirche* (Nordengenblätter 1924).
5. Everyman Edition, pp. 51–2.
6. Sonderausgabe, p. 703, Eng. tr. (The Marxist Library), p. 292 f.
7. 'Introduction to a Critique of Hegel's Philosophy of Law', an early essay of Marx in *Deutsch-Französische Jahrbücher* (1844), opening pages.
8. Hans Prinzhorn, *Psychotherapy: A Search for Essentials*, Eng. tr. (London 1935), p. 31.
9. (London 1944).
10. (Oxford 1949).
11. L. Feuerbach, *Das Wesen des Christentums* (Leipzig 1841).
12. Auguste Comte, *Catéchisme Positiviste* (Paris 1891), 6e entretien, p. 162.
13. I should add that 'spirit' is here used to denote man's inner principle, by which he *affects* Nature, and which is not therefore the equivalent of what is 'spiritual' in the sense of morally good or religious or godly, i.e. orientated towards God.
14. T. H. Buckle, *History of Civilization* (1857 and 1861), World's Classics ed., vol. I, p. 140.

CHAPTER VI

The Debate about Human Nature

★

What is the proper estimate of man's nature? This question is raised in a specialized form by the rise and decline of capitalism, and the socialism which is at once its heir and opponent. 'Nature' in this question connotes neither man's share in the physical and biological realm, nor his *natura*, that is his specifically human constitution which distinguishes him from mineral, animal and vegetative creatures on the one hand, and from angelic and divine beings on the other. Nature in the phrase 'human nature' is man's actual condition. This, in the language of theology, represents the interaction between man's participation in the sub-human realm and his spiritual centre with its superiority to Nature and his power to subdue it; it also includes the power to violate his *natura*; and to respond to or oppose or disregard the supernatural ground of his being.

In connection with the upheavals of modern social history the question of 'human nature' is predominantly an inquiry as to whether in man's actual condition the self-regarding or the altruistic impulse is the deeper. Never has there been such a confused debate—so confused that anyone who has the temerity to offer some clarification must do so in fear and trembling lest he should be found in the ditch more blind than those he wishes to guide. Let us list a few of the confusions. For one thing, in close relation to our subject, it is widely assumed that defenders of capitalism hold the self-regarding impulse to be the deeper—and that their criticisms of collectivist programmes rest upon conviction that man is not good enough for socialism. Actually the great radicals who

The Debate about Human Nature

heralded the economy of capitalism and the free market system believed that the social principle was so deep in reality that it lay outside man's self altogether—that a providential order used even his vices for a harmonious end—as we find in extreme form in Mandeville's *Fable of the Bees*. At a later stage liberals and socialists alike tended to condemn a low view of human nature, for that view is supposed in their eyes to be a factor of resistance in the way of a co-operative commonwealth. But a number of the most pertinent critics of the free-market economy and the capitalist organization which it used have made their criticism on the ground that this unrestricted economic scramble assumed too high a view of human nature. It posited in human motives an independence of social conditioning, it assumed an altruism that would spread to unknown persons in a vast network of impersonal economic relations, it presumed upon a willing mobility in men and their families which would make for economic equilibrium by sending them wherever employment and income inducements seemed to demand. In brief, there have been as many and as strong motives for espousing a socialist order because of man's evil, his fallibility and limitations, as there have been on the ground that it presupposed a perfectibility which capitalism had seemed to deny. It cannot be maintained that capitalism and socialism are to be distinguished by their separate assumptions about the actual badness or goodness of man. Both estimates of human nature are to be found in upholders of both economies. Robert Owen himself discovered the reason why many experiments in voluntary socialism failed, because, in his own words, 'men are not morally prepared for socialism'. Nicholas Berdyaev condemns bourgeois capitalism for presupposing too exalted a view of human nature. We have already looked at some evidence that the intellectual sponsors of *laissez-faire* economics held mistaken views of the altruistic and community motives in men, believing them to underlie every and any economic superstructure. 'The *laissez-faire* system did not in fact eliminate moral purpose,' writes E. H. Carr. He shows that for two centuries the doctrine of the natural harmony of interests could be maintained for two specific historical reasons. One was that 'notwithstanding the philosophic premises of liberal demo-

The Debate about Human Nature

cracy and *laissez-faire*, self-sacrifice for moral (and community) purposes, though eliminated in theory, continued to be practised and even preached as a private and social virtue'. It might be argued that 'the ingrained and irrational habits of personal abstinence and public service, associated with the puritan tradition, played a more important part in building up the liberal and *laissez-faire* society of the nineteenth century than the rational morality of the harmony of interests'.[1] The second reason for the temporary success of this creed is, of course, that expanding markets and increased production did create higher standards of consumption right through the social scale, and so appeared to be a permanent community benefit. And J. M. Clark put the point rather more cynically: 'The strongest basis for individualism is not the intelligence of individuals and their irrevocable devotion to the pursuit of their own self-interest but rather their stupidity and their susceptibility to moral suggestion.'[2] There is plenty of evidence that the philosophic radicals, and especially those of them who made the theory of evolutionary naturalism their warrant for liberalism in economics, had read into the evolutionary process they envisaged, the moral and social virtues they stood for as men of the European cultural tradition.[3] Herbert Spencer's essay in *Evolutionary Ethics* is one of the more naïve examples.[4]

It is to be noticed that while the secular thinkers took the view that harmony was inherent in economy, the religious force which, if it did not give birth to, at any rate certainly gave a good conscience to, the growth of the mercenary dispositions, namely Calvinism, was pessimistic in its attitude to human nature. 'Calvinism', says a modern writer, 'was the religious movement which accepted frankly the new situation. Its theology starts from the idea that the whole world is corrupt. Everything man does by his own strength is sin, and original sin is identified with human nature as a whole.' And here is the really interesting remark: 'The Puritans tried to overcome the sense of guilt by achieving holiness. This paradox—for holiness cannot be achieved on this theological premise—led to a combination of *mass asceticism* and the reality of the struggle of man against man in a capitalist society.'[5] The mass asceticism disappeared, but the struggle remained. This

The Debate about Human Nature

struggle which gave its character to the capitalist phase, especially in its decline, was the one element in society upon which the communist theorists fastened in their revolt against the optimism or idealism, as they called it, of the liberal democratic outlook.

However we may estimate the relation of Calvinist Predestination and modern industrial capitalism, and the idea of the Calling as the dynamic principle behind the use of the commercial era, it is worth noting that one result of the connection is still with us. It is the disposition to regard economic activity as a refuge from a sense of guilt—a kind of alibi for loss of salvation in the more direct personal relation of man to God as well as man to man. By relying upon a purely subjective principle, namely the calling to man to spend himself in a process without any such criticism of the process as can be gleaned from a conception of the total nature of man, he is left with the impulse to intensify his activity as a pledged sign of grace, without regard to the result. Where economic activity is consecrated as an interior discipline, then if success in labour of hand and brain makes effort less and less necessary—or if men want a simpler life for their souls' good—then as producers and traders they are steadily deprived of the spiritual medicine they have relied on.

That was a parenthesis as a reminder that the doctrine of economic man and the near achievement of that creature who is still with us under capitalism and socialism—have their parentage in an optimistic secular theory and a pessimistic religious one.

But the optimistic secular view has opposite political results: '*Laissez-faire* without the belief in perfectibility yields the conservatism of Burke or of the later Wordsworth; with that belief it produces the liberalism of Priestley and the nineteenth century—though even from this standpoint you might have first to remove obstacles in order that nature might function freely. Lastly—and this is the creed of revolution—one might treat nature as dross to be moulded in our own likeness, we must alter rather than explain. . . .'[6]

We have now reached a provisional, though somewhat negative, conclusion, namely that high and low estimates of human nature are to be found in defenders of both capitalist and socialist systems.

The Debate about Human Nature

The main difference, as a rough generalization, is that believers in the free-market economy held that the community principle lay underneath man's efforts and would bend them to a social purpose (what they counted on was the social cement of natural groups *and* a civilized tradition), whereas the socialist pioneers in the West held that the harmonies had to be created by man himself—presupposing of course that the socialist planners had hold of a deeper element in reality than the chaos of economic struggle. This too was attached early to an evolutionary view, in which the goal of social harmony was held to be backed up by the cosmic march of things. Marx and Lenin introduced a revolutionary principle into this scheme, without abandoning the backing that social evolution gave to the struggle for a completely co-operative society. And when the revolution is complete, then the state of man will be exactly what the liberal optimists said it was already. So in one way or another, at first, second or third remove, all these estimates of man, the *laissez-faire* one, the democratic socialist one and the Marxist-communist one, are at bottom estimates made by 'the children of light', in Reinhold Niebuhr's use of the Biblical phrase to describe those who innocently ignore the fundamental contradiction in man and his tragic effort to overcome it on the human plane alone.[7]

The debate about human nature has been equally confused since the sixteenth century on the general question whether man is ultimately more of an individualist or community fellow. Because men observed the striving for individual fulfilment in that modern age they often mistook this second nature for man's essential *natura*. Then they observed that after a certain point, when the pre-Enlightenment stock of community dispositions underneath the age of enterprise was beginning to run low, people sought to recreate a social reality out of the dissociated elements and tended to regard the competitive impulses in economic life as an aberration. The confusion is made mightily worse when the untheological Christian comes into the debate and fastens on one side of the polarity in man's *natura*—the polarity of community and individual—and proceeds to equate the one most badly needed in the modern situation with the supernatural charity of the realm of

The Debate about Human Nature

grace, and the other with the old Adam, or the pull of material nature, or the invasion of the evil one into man's habitation. The fact is that both the community and the individualist propensities are part of man's *natura* in dialectical interplay; or to put the contrast on another level, man's immersion in and his over-against attitude towards, his natural and social setting. The redemptive power of Christianity does not set one against the other, but enables a supernatural altruism to arise on top of their natural pulls upon man. But short of that—there is to be found an interpretation of man which comes out of the Christian experience of redemption, an interpretation which allows the believer to detect the idolatrous nature of one pole in the dialectic if it is given absolute value as the link of man with the absolute, and to demand in the name of the *natural man* that such and such changes in the social order are required for him the better to lead his human life. The form such changes will take will always be relative to the particular misbalance at the moment, and will be a counter-movement to either the idolatry of absolute individualism or absolute collectivism. There is, that is to say, a Christian doctrine of the secular order as well as of the realm of grace. This is represented by the birds that come to roost in the mustard tree of the Kingdom of God. The tree's purpose is to bear its own fruit, but it performs a sub-ordinate function as well.

To prepare the ground for such an interpretation, let us see how the Christian weight might be put in the present debate about human nature. The secular theorists have their own fun out of it. Here is Lord Shaftesbury chiding Hobbes's view of man as an aggressive egoist: 'Sir! The Philosophy you have condescended to reveal to us is most extraordinary. We are beholden to you for your instruction. But, pray, whence is this zeal on our behalf? What are we to you? . . . Is there such a thing as natural affections? If not, why all the pains—of what advantage is it to you to deliver us from the cheat.'[8] In contrast to this playfulness we have the sombre Oswald Spengler declaring that man is a beast of prey, and yet counselling him to take an heroic stand with fate—and so the paradox is repeated again and again. But it is of more importance to see that the free enterprise and individual fulfilment of the modern period partly rest upon the community consciousness inherited from earlier ones and is also a kind of compensation for the loss of it. An American expert on business administration and personnel, F. J. Roethligsberger, holds that our industrial civilization of the present is improvidently living on its capital, upon the store of human goodwill and 'self-abnegation that many centuries of established routine of living have left us'. He finds on the lower levels of administration 'men of extraordinary skill in the direction of securing co-operative effort. This gift is too little recognized, because technical competence wins recognition and promotion whereas skill in handling human relations does not. Yet if it were not for these men the unleashed forces of modern technology would pour themselves out to doom and destruction.'[9] And the late Elton Mayo, Professor of Industrial Research at Harvard, found that among industrial workers or university students the proportionate number actuated 'by motives of self-interest logically elaborated is exceedingly small. *They have relapsed upon self-interest when social association has failed them.*' He adds: 'it would seem that extensive social disorganization must be postulated before the so-called laws of economics apply. In other words, our studies of economic fact are upside down; we have, as it were, an extensive pathology, but no physiology, an elaborate study of abnormal social determinations, none of the normal.'[10]

The Hammonds refer to de Quincey in connection with the transformation of personal Jacobinism, which is part of the natural man, into political and economic self-assertion, which was colossally induced by the break-up of social groupings in the industrial age. De Quincey and his brother, at the beginning of the last century, when on their way to school in Manchester, used to meet a number of mill boys who called them 'bucks' and pelted them with stones because they wore hessian boots. De Quincey adds that however angry they were made by his aristocratic dress, the youths from the mill had no sympathy with political Jacobinism and would shout readily enough for Church and King. Their personal Jacobinism he explained, was 'of that sort which is native to the heart of man, who is by natural impulse (and not without a root of nobility, although also of base envy) impatient of inequality, and submits

The Debate about Human Nature

to it only through a sense of its necessity, or under long experience of its benefits'. The Hammonds comment that by 1830 a political Jacobinism was developing, due to the offer that the industrial revolution was making to men as a compensation for their loss of community feeling. It offered the poor man the prospect of ceasing to be a poor man, by his own diligence and worth. 'It offered the poor man something to touch his imagination.'[11]

To return to the outline of a Christian doctrine of the secular order, with special reference to this question, we observe that the debate about human motives usually comes into the issue of capitalism and socialism in some such way as this. Defenders of the free-market system say: Socialism has always failed in the past, and is bound to fail in the future because it makes demands upon human nature to which mankind in the mass will not respond; it might work in a society of angels. Socialist and communist writers affirm that when 'communal ownership of the means of production' is achieved, human nature will change, men will work as hard for the socialist commonwealth as they will work for themselves and for their families. When the one uses religious language, he declares that the only possible means of freeing men from self-regarding motives is redeeming grace which enables them to act from disinterested love for God and man, and that reformers have forgotten the Fall of Man. The other holds that the self-regarding impulses are not inherent in men on earth and that they have been induced by a defective social order and in particular by the conflict of interest in different economic classes.

The Christian moralist recognizes a distinct state of life known as holiness in which the sanctified man does act from the supernatural motive of charity (or *caritas*, to distinguish it from the debased usage of 'charity' for kindness to the unfortunate) and in this state he disregards all self-regarding or self-expressive motives, however low or high they may be, when they conflict with it. But he does not, therefore, lump together as on the same level all the non-religious human motives in the bare category of man's sinfulness. Certainly, with the sense of his own imperfection and looking from the point where he knows what supernatural charity means, he can say with Kierkegaard, before God men are always in the

The Debate about Human Nature

wrong, or with Isaiah, all our righteousnesses are as a polluted garment. But with this insight, when the Christian moralist moves from attention to the realm of grace to that of ethics, he does recognize real and valid moral differences within the field of non-supernatural and relatively interested motives. He knows the Fall of Man to mean that men, himself included, commonly act from a variety of motives from the most exalted to the most base, still within the sphere of self-interest or self-expression, and as such distinct from the sphere of grace. But on their own side of the line there are moral differences between such motives. It is on this level that he approaches the debate about human nature in the social transitions of our time.

It is a peculiar feature of the capitalist and post-capitalist world that the only motive generally considered as the opposite of complete altruism is the desire for economic gain for oneself or family. Love of neighbour and economic self-interest are the two contradictories in the modern economic age. But in the history of man and even in the interstices of bourgeois economic relations there are found many other motives determining a man's attitude to what he does; they are not altruistic and they are not gainful. One of these we have already appealed to a good deal, namely a natural community sense, reaching from a kind of human gregariousness to the desire for the good opinion of one's fellows and of the opposite sex. Another is interest in the well-doing of the work in hand, the craftsman's pride in the job. A third is a seeking of power and prestige, and a fourth is the conviction of having some kind of social or world mission. In varying degrees these impulses have moved men to and often kept them in occupations which they could have exchanged for more profitable ones. Also, within any society that does not rely upon compulsion, different motives are at work in different classes; and men change their motives when they move from one to another. As Mannheim observes: 'The proletariat works mainly in order to earn a living, while the middle classes, once their primary wants have been supplied and their need for security satisfied, work mainly for the sake of increased power and prestige.... The group we call the intelligentsia is actuated mainly by motives of its own. A member of this

The Debate about Human Nature

group is only happy when he has work which is in keeping with his special interests and qualifications. . . . Whenever a man rises to a higher class, from unskilled labourer to skilled labourer, from small tradesman to large-scale *entrepreneur*, from petty officialdom to a learned profession, once in the ranks of the *élite* he switches over from one set of motives to another.'[12]

Moreover, the dominance of one set of motives in one period changes over to another set at a later stage. We considered in the earlier lectures how economic motives gained a dominance in the era of rising capitalism. It was also observed that the 'spirit of enterprise' of the trading and then of the productive developments was a spirit inherited from chivalric, exploring, travelling and buccaneering habits—in brief, from pre-capitalist dispositions. The spirit of enterprise inaugurated capitalism and carried it on for some of its history; but also the culture formed by the industrial age began to extinguish this spirit, which has given place to dispositions seeking security, social services, amenities and administrative rather than entrepreneurial occupations. From both ends of the social scale there has been an approach to a middle-class mode of life.[13] But what, in the decline of capitalism, remains from its ascendancy, is the disposition to satisfy the demands of social recognition and prestige in terms of commodity hedonism. That presents the reforming socialist ideal in a post-capitalist world with something of a dilemma. That ideal is ready to slow up the rate of material progress for the sake of more human and fraternal social relations, when its preachers have the insight to see that a real choice of these alternatives has to be made and the courage to say so. But the commodity hedonism which capitalism has transmitted to its socialist heirs demands just what only a larger stream of technically-made products can give.

That, however, is by the way. The point I am now making is that the motives which induce or impel men to enter co-operatively into the economic process vary with the cultural atmosphere of a period and with the social stratum of the individuals concerned. All of these motives are self-interested in a wide, and not by any means always in a despicable sense. Some of them are much more socially orientated than others. The question whether

The Debate about Human Nature

a social system counts on men acting for self-regarding gain or possibly changing over to the selflessness of archangels, is therefore quite beside the point. A Christian judgement upon the workability and relative justice of a particular social order does not ask whether it presupposes supernatural love in its members or self-regarding egoism in men or groups. It keeps in its accounts a separate moral balance sheet which shows an unpayable debt with regard to the claims of disinterested charity. And this situation has to be dealt with in the economy of grace and salvation. But keeping this balance sheet always before itself, it then confronts the world's balance sheet which it sets in different terms. There the claims of supernatural charity do not appear; instead there are a great number of self-interested motives of varying degrees of egoism and altruism, and it is those whose relative strengths have to be assessed. In other words, Christian judgement on a social order examines how far its structure and culture foster the more egoistical or the more altruistic self-interested motives; and when sometimes self-interestedness is inclined to be altruistic it asks, what kind of good—real or illusory—does it seek to spread to others? We will now elaborate something of this Christian judgement on the secular order.

First, be it noted that self-interest is not a single motive always directed to gain and power at the expense of others. There have been many expressions of the view that all actions are self-regarding and that this is always ego-centric. Here is one of the most lively in recent literature.

On a bitter snowy night a man had given his car fare away to an old ragged woman and so had to walk three miles home in the cold. He did this, says Mark Twain in a curious little book, out of self-interest, for had he not done it he would have been tormented with a bad conscience. 'He bought a whole night's sleep—all for twenty-five cents.'[14] That is Mark Twain's sharp way of saying that all good actions are done for those kinds of self-satisfaction which are disguised forms of egoism.

Others have maintained that what we call good and bad are only names for what is in our self-interest or against it. Then some moralists have answered that if self-interest enters at all into the

The Debate about Human Nature

doing of an act, then it cannot be a morally good act. The main tradition of Christian ethics rejects both these points of view. It holds that an action is good when it responds to an obligation which is other than increasing one's satisfaction; only because men do not in their sinful state naturally want the good, the doing of it goes against the grain and requires moral effort; we then become conscious of a sense of duty at war with our desires—as when we resist anger or keep a promise to our hurt. But, on the other hand, Christian teaching will not allow that an action ceases to be morally good just because it may give satisfaction to the doer of it; it is possible to do the right thing and find that it does not conflict with our self-interest—as when I enjoy my dinner, or pull my weight in a team, or please my wife, or do a job that interests me, or say my prayers when they are going well. Of course, the moral life means that I do these things even when I am not inclined to them; but they are none the less good when they are backed up by real desire.

Now, it is the conflict between acting for our own advantage and that of others which presents the most familiar form of the question. It looks as if our self-regarding sentiments must be opposed to concern for other people, as frequently they are. But notice that when Christ repeated the old law: 'Thou shalt love thy neighbour as thyself', it assumes that there is a right way of loving oneself—whether we take the words to mean we should love the neighbour as we love ourself, or because he is such an one as ourself. The great Christian teacher, St. Augustine, when he said: 'Love and do what you like', shocked some people who did not realize that at a certain religious level, where a man had really learned to act spontaneously and consistently out of love for God and man, then there was no conflict between his charity and what he wanted to do. Read again the 119th Psalm. There you will catch the experience of one for whom it is a struggle to do the holy will, but who has fleeting knowledge of the joy that it is to have his desires and his duty at one, and longs for this to be a permanent state. 'O that my ways were made so direct that I might keep thy statutes! So shall I not be confounded.'

We can put it like this. The goal of religious faith and discipline

The Debate about Human Nature

is the state where that which is satisfying to the self is found to be at one with our love of God and our fellows. That is the joy of the saints. But also, short of that, in the midst of our imperfect life, where to do the good mostly means a struggle with our desires, there are times when the good act is also the one which pleases us —it is not in conflict with our self-interest. Or, to put it in another way, we must distinguish two kinds of self-interest, one which is only self-regarding and opposed to our concern for others; another kind which goes along with our desire for the good of other people.

I want now to consider variations in this second kind of self-interest—generous self-interest shall we call it—in their bearing upon the practicability and desirability of different social orders, such as capitalism and socialism. The question comes up in this way. Goodwill towards men is surely shown when we wish more of them to have the benefits conferred upon us or upon the more fortunate by our civilization. It looks then as if all that is needed to ensure the growth and maintenance of a good social structure is an extended and deepened altruism, that is to say a concern that all others shall enjoy what does, or what we hope will, give us abiding satisfaction. In an earlier lecture we considered how a civilized organization of life acquires a direction of its own which is not by any means the same as the best aims of men at one period want it to be. And now I wish to emphasize that a civilization often induces in us men a deceptive idea of what our real selves really want. Haven't you often gone on doing things, even when you were not compelled, after you really wanted to stop. I have more than once heard it said: 'I'm fed up with the pictures, but what else is there to do?' And I find myself reading trivial bits of the papers—even advertisements, when it bores me and keeps me from what I would really want to be doing. It is that our civilization induces certain habits and desires, which we do not positively will to follow. They are part of the climate in which we live, they cling round our souls as a sort of bogus good we had better not miss.

These may not be very important matters. We have earlier alluded to more serious ones, showing that a particular culture gives men notions of what is for the human good, which may be

The Debate about Human Nature

very deceptive. The railway and the steamship have been net gain to human communities. But with the motor car and the aeroplane, along with the satisfactions they give, numerous disadvantages arise which have to be offset against the satisfactions. I refer to traffic problems, knocking about of villages and towns, noise, the taking of good land badly needed for food and houses, material wanted for good furniture, increase of restless mobility, less care for the place we live in, encouragement to divide sharply places where men live and where they work. Instead of linking communities those developments tend to disintegrate them. But men's sense of what is for the benefit of a greater number is largely formed by these tendencies, uncritically accepted.

We considered, too, how industrial development enriches a community which is sound in its agriculture, its domestic and craft life, and in its spiritual robustness. But beyond a certain point it ceases to be an enrichment and begins to weaken natural association between men, and even begins to endanger instead of raising the standard of living. But it is not easy to stop an overdevelopment for it has a momentum of its own, and it becomes more difficult when its vocal representatives regard it as constituting civilization and thousands of human beings get their living in it. Moreover, certain notions of what is social betterment, derived from this momentum, inform the minds of men. Whether I am right or wrong in detail about these tendencies, the problem is a serious reminder that when we are trying to be altruistic, we have not only to find out whether the good we wish extended to others is really the human good and not what our civilization persuades us to think it is, but also whether the benefits of our civilization can be reproduced for our descendants—or whether we are using up the capital of our culture regardless of the future, perhaps even thinking we are making sacrifices for it.

There is another aspect to this question of well-directed or misdirected altruism. We do not realize sufficiently that it is possible to increase the civilized equipment of life, which we believe in for others as well as ourselves, at the expense of impoverishing the inner resources of men. Then they become unhappy and frustrated however much civilization gives them. Take this case which comes

The Debate about Human Nature

close to me as a teacher. Our civilization was formed by a growth of traditions, beliefs, institutions and modes of living, handed down from one generation to another. It discovered at one stage that knowledge, in the sense of information, was a powerful help in coping with life. Knowledge helped wisdom. But we have now reached a stage when it is supposed that an increase of knowledge will give wisdom. Just to have information poured at you from all directions does not deepen your powers of discernment or judgement. These come from the arts of life learnt from a continuous tradition which one has imbibed, and *then* perhaps confronted critically with other schools of thought. But what are we to say about the myriad facts, impressions and views people now get from a day's newspapers, radio programmes and discussion talks without end. There may be a hundred best books to read, as there were in my youth published by an enterprising firm, but you did not get a hundred times more understanding by reading them all than by reading one. To try to live by the outlook of one of them and reflect upon the result brings more wisdom than the attempt to know what they all say. The point of this illustration is to question the assumption to-day that more information about things and views makes for understanding. Yet our civilization encourages this assumption, because it is good at devising mass-production methods for dispensing such knowledge, and 'the children of light' believe that the more information and impressions are made to bear upon people the nearer they will be to self-fulfilment.

What I've been getting at is the need to question not only the self-regarding motives of men and groups, but also the things we have come to take for granted as in the human interest. We are so much the heirs of our particular civilization—we think this is what normal humanity is—that it requires spiritual and mental effort to stand a bit outside it and examine the aims it predisposes men to pursue. We have, for instance, in these parts of the world come to regard economic status as the supreme good and loss of it as a terrible calamity. But all peoples do not feel that way. The suicide rate among failures in the economic climb is higher among Anglo-Saxon peoples than among Southerners, for whom economic status is not of such momentous consequence. Assumptions vary even

The Debate about Human Nature

about what is social value. With us it is largely the increase of economic assets; some native peoples of North America and elsewhere take satisfaction and acquire status by giving wealth away lavishly and even destroying it with display.

It is necessary then to realize that the things we assume to be the good for ourselves and others are often misleading and the ideas only induced by our particular civilized mode of life. Renewal will mean revising these notions by a standard which we bring to our judgement from other sources, namely from religious and educational traditions which operate from a deeper insight into human nature and its real needs than this or that civilized pattern contains within it. That is why the health of a civilization requires that its religion, its ethics and its teaching lore stand for the universal and essential truths about man and his destiny and do not merely reflect the notions of a particular society about what is the good life.

It seems then that we cannot account for human behaviour in society by a comparison between bare altruistic or bare self-regarding motives; nor can we describe social systems with any illumination by trying to assess how far they rely predominantly upon one or other of these features of human character; and certainly we cannot judge the validity in the truly human interest of, say, capitalist society and collectivism, by attaching one to a genial and the other to a severe estimate of man's moral and social dispositions, or by criticizing one of them for having a false account of human nature. Having tried to correct this over-simplified statement of the problem as one of egoism versus altruism, I wish to get out of the way two common attitudes which seem to present the question wrongly from the start. You often hear it said, especially by idealist Christians, that if you want better systems you must make better men; or, if men would live by disinterested love there would be no need to change the system. This statement is so true that it is not worth uttering. If it means anything, it is a categorical statement that the Kingdom of Heaven is independent of social systems; indeed, if all men acted in society by the unadulterated love of God and man, there would be no need to change the system, for there would be no system. For example, a social

The Debate about Human Nature

order using the law which is a device for preventing egoism from destroying society, or putting prices on efforts and goods, which makes a sort of guarantee that people can count on a *quid pro quo*, or moved by the effective but unorganized deterrents of a slanging from the old lady next door—this social *order* is there at all because men do not and cannot act in all their relations by unambiguous love and the confidence that the others will do the same. The system represents the positive associative expression of man's social nature taking a hand in preventing man's self-regarding impulses from destroying human existence. That is not the whole truth about the social order. There is also organization, e.g. for exchange of letters, due to our finiteness and limitation, and not to our evil. I should doubt though whether even letter-writing would be required in the Kingdom of Heaven! And in social organizations there are positive aims for a certain kind of civilization and not only for social survival. But even here it is man's unfulfilled life during his pilgrimage on earth that seeks civilization as a kind of surrogate for the Kingdom of God. My point is that a social system is the result of interaction between man's alienation from his true self on the one hand and the pull from behind of his essential nature on the other, which seeks to overcome the alienation. A good system is therefore not one that presumes upon human perfectibility, but one which best serves to make a frame in an imperfect world for the associative forces the better to counteract the dissociative ones.

A kindred question arises in connection with the vast power which modern techniques, physical, political and psychological, put into the hands of men, used by men over Nature, used by governments over citizens, used by some purveyors of ideas over many people. It is said that power is neutral, that it all depends upon the use men make of it, whether its results are a blessing or a curse. But no! It is not like that; human beings are not as unconditioned by the tools they use as this assumes. Take two cases. Mechanical and chemical aids are used in getting easier results out of the effort. Because this works well in a measure, a vast vested interest grows up in extending this process, and it soon becomes well-nigh impossible to call a halt because it means disemploying a population. The instruments of power call for their increase, even

The Debate about Human Nature

if wisdom decides that a proper balance has been upset. The same goes for physical energy in production, when it is discovered that beyond a certain point its very efficiency may have destroyed a social pattern the stability of which was one of the incentives to work it. The principle is most clear in the use of genocidal weapons. The most humane peoples will resort to these things only as a last resort. Governments unscrupulous about preservation of life in their own peoples, and about limitation of military methods by any code of war, such governments will have the advantage. Be that as it may, wise statesmanship does not consist in welcoming any and every development of power, assuming that man is free to make it serviceable or destructive. Statesmanship consists in knowing how, man being what he is always and in this situation, power can be used, distributed or curbed, the better to bring the good out of the evil in it. We can notice lately a new note in the voice of those who applaud every addition to man's power over Nature and his fellow men. Whereas they used to complain that ethics were irrelevant or even reactionary, now they tend to get angry with the moralist and the Churches for not having effectively perfected human nature so that it can be relied upon to protect technical progress from becoming humanly harmful. So much for the error of perfectibility; it usually leads to some kind of hell.

Christian realism is equally critical of the view which would rely exclusively upon an altruistic sense of duty or love, as it is of one which denies wholesale the real impulses of association and community. It will counter theories which hold that removal of exploitation or a change of system will reveal human nature in its pristine altruistic beauty, and it will likewise counter the cynicism which holds the race to be a collection of egoists which require holding together by gain or compulsion. The picture which emerges from a Christian estimate of human nature is something like this. Man by his very being is a community fellow; he partakes of the ultimate solidarity of things. But there is an evil principle at work which disrupts community. 'Our sinful world', wrote Berdyaev, 'is the scene of a conflict between opposed forces; this conflict determines the existence of the organic universe; it is a fact of the social world of man and would seem also to be carried on in the world of spirits good and evil.'[15] This force of conflict goes very deep, but it does not go all the way. 'An enemy hath done this', it says in the parable of the wheat and the tares. Evil is not ultimate. Therefore—and this is the third heading in the Christian scheme—it is possible for men involved in the egoisms of this world to be so infused with the grace of God that they become almost entirely other-regarding. But that is sanctity, not politics. And my friend D. R. Davies has good grounds for defining politics as 'deferred repentance'. But now, of these three things, the ultimate unity, the evil that disrupts it, and the sanctity that recovers it in the redeemed life, of these three history knows only the middle one. But it knows something else too; it knows that the pull of mankind's original righteousness, as it were, leads him, even far short of sanctity, to recover a replica of true community, still in the sinful order. This makes in the main two kinds of groupings; communities of men who share common roots, and associations of men who find a unity in common purposes. Culture or common purpose is a corrective of the dissociative force of sin. The pull of common interests, the bond created by a team effort, is the principle of the most vital form of human association though its power is usually ignored by the politician and reformer. Solidarities like these come time and again with little binding machinery when common interests of livelihood, culture, civilization or religion have been induced. To will society is not to will to be social but to will what others will. Men do not think about brotherhood when they are acting in a common effort, they think about the job. In a fallen world friendship and love and fellowship all break down at some point for two reasons, and this breakdown is often surmounted by an interest or purpose above them which can tide the parties over the collapse of purely mutual regard. The two reasons are that to one man, he not being God, the individuality of the other remains an unfathomable mystery, and that owing to sin the natural man does not love disinterestedly. But through the mediation of the common thing, association and a measure of community are possible. Of course, even these solidarities are invaded by egoism, as Reinhold Niebuhr has done most to remind us: 'Every immediate loyalty is a potential danger to higher and more inclusive loyalties and an opportunity for the expression of a sublimated egoism.'[16] In other words, the socially disruptive forces in man feed on his very associations; that is one of the causes of the frailty of civilization. Its conflicts are more violent, deep-cutting and disruptive as civilization advances, because the anti-social impulses of man are more hidden than in direct man to man relationships.

I must not pursue this further. We have to get back to our theme with this fact clearly in mind; forms of social structure are to be judged not by assessment of bare egoism and altruism, but by the extent to which this or that form tends to foster or destroy those natural and purposive associations by which imperfect man produces a reflection of true community. Remember Elton Mayo's saying, which I think has caught the Christian psychology of the matter: 'They have relapsed upon self-interest when social association has failed them.' I have repeated, perhaps to weariness, that the age which gave such prominence to economic motives could count for a time on these other associative impulses and then tended to undermine them. So it began to look as if man was moved entirely by pecuniary and business concerns. But it is not so. Some of you may know the passage in Mr. Belloc's book *The Path to Rome*, where he tells of a man trundling a large vat of wine about on a cart and haggling for the price of it; in the end he hands out drinks all round for nothing. Which only shows, says the author, that what man most wants is not gain, but his own way. And here, from a less picturesque setting, is a high-business administrator, Mr. Chester Barnard, President of the New Jersey Bell Telephone Company. In a book, *The Function of the Executives*, he writes: 'Though I early found out how to behave effectively in organizations, not until I had much later relegated economic theory and economic interests to a secondary—though indispensable—place did I begin to understand organizations or human behaviour in them.' Many of us know how men who now need a good deal of inducement to work through the organization of industrial society, would in an emergency like bombing in war-time turn their skills to patching things up for anybody about who needed it, without concern for gain or even for recognition. Work is still done just because it needs to be done; many would gladly

The Debate about Human Nature

do better work than the system allows them to do; prestige often counts for more than remuneration. Above all, status in work seems to be an elemental need which no modern industrial society has succeeded in according to the mass of men. Instead, apart from compulsions, they are bidden to consider the good of the whole, and the state only seems to know what that is. Mr. Maurice Reckitt has insisted that for the conditions of work to call out the natural associative impulses of men, that work must be not only a ministry, something done for the community; it must also be a vocation, done for the good of the work itself; and it must be a partnership, a partnership not only in the proceeds but also in ownership and responsibility. I would add that these conditions are not fulfilled by nationalized industries, and I would also add that such a partnership must be sensed as a reality on a wet Monday morning (to use Mr. Nigel Balchin's phrase) and not only when fired (if that is the right word) to collective enthusiasm when reading the *New Statesman*.

There is something in our industrial civilization that has tended to destroy the associative propensities of men; then it looks as if the social problem is one between the egoistic and altruistic motives. It is in our day that the problem of incentives has come to the fore. This arises when economic bonds have replaced most of the other kinds of bond—and then when the spur of economic advancement seems like a wild-goose chase. It is in such conditions that people tend to act purely from self-interest and at worst become social delinquents. It is a sure sign of social disintegration when men have to be nagged into being co-operative. Oscar Wilde sensed this when he declared, as he said he believed, that the great advantage of socialism was that it would relieve us of the sordid necessity of living for others. It might be answered that a state socialism that finds no way of re-creating associations in which men satisfy their co-operative instincts does not even do that. If the average human being does not find status, community and significance where he is, namely for the most part in his work and in his home, then no substitute incentive such as the prestige of belonging to a superior culture or industrial society in an otherwise doomed world will save him from deepened frustrations.

The Debate about Human Nature

It is written in the Epistle of St. James: 'Whence come war and whence come fightings among you? Come they not hence, even of your desires that war in your members?' There are depicted not primarily hateful, aggressive or rivalrous motives, but interior demands and conflicts which lead to rivalry. St. James shows that conflict between men is an attempt to solve an interior problem by external means. Dissension between persons and groups is the product of internal disorders. A later teacher, St. Thomas Aquinas, makes a useful distinction between concord and peace, a distinction marked in the Mattins collect of the Prayer Book, where God is spoken of as the author of peace and the lover of concord. St. Thomas says: 'Concord, properly speaking, is between one man and another, in so far as the will of various hearts agree together in consenting to the same thing. Now the heart of one man may tend to diverse things . . . in so far as one and the same appetitive power tends to diverse objects which it cannot obtain all at the same time. Now the union of such movements is essential to peace.'[17] This is to say that without a right ordering of human life within the soul or within a social group there will be no peace. The disturbances within the parts then make the boundaries between the parts lines along which conflict gathers. The false order of living within one part makes for aggressiveness between the parts.

I have sought to establish that when the natural associative elements are denied proper scope, men are thrown upon self-regarding forms of behaviour. This estimate will save us from the shallow optimism which believes human nature to be so perfectible that we need not bother about the structure of society, and equally from the deadening cynicism that holds man to be so much of an egoist that he has to be enticed by gain or fitted with a collectivist strait-jacket.

NOTES

1. E. H. Carr, *Conditions of Peace* (London 1942), chap. V.
2. J. M. Clark, *The Trend of Economics*, p. 97. Quoted in E. H. Carr, Ibid, p. 104.
3. See Wm. F. Guillian, Junr., *The Moral Theory of Evolutionary Naturalism* (Yale 1945).

The Debate about Human Nature

4. Herbert Spencer, *Various Fragments* (London 1879).
5. Bruno Meier, chapter on 'Moral Sanctions' in *Christianity and the Social Revolution* (London 1935), pp. 403 ff.
6. Basil Willey, *The Eighteenth Century Background* (London 1949), p. 206.
7. Reinhold Niebuhr, *The Children of Light and the Children of Darkness* (London 1945).
8. Shaftesbury, *Essay on the Freedom of Wit and Humour*, Works vol. I, p. 91. Quoted in Basil Willey, op. cit., p. 68.
9. F. J. Roethligsberger, 'The Foreman, Master and Victim of Double Talk', *Harvard Business Review*, vol. XXIII (Harvard 1945), p. 294.
10. Elton Mayo, *The Social Problems of an Industrial Civilization* (Harvard 1945), p. 43.
11. J. L. and Barbara Hammond, *The Bleak Age*, p. 42 f.
12. Karl Mannheim, *Man and Society* (London 1940), pp. 315-16.
13. 'The bourgeois style of dress, the bourgeois habit of saving, a bourgeois house—these are the goals of the British working man's endeavours.'—B. de Jouvenel, *Problems of Socialist England* (London 1949), p. 126.
14. Mark Twain, *What is Man?* (London 1937), pp. 14 ff.
15. N. Berdyaev, *Christianity and Class War* (London 1933), chap. I.
16. R. Niebuhr, *Moral Man and Immoral Society* (New York 1932).
17. *Summa Theologica*, II, ii, Q.29, 1 and 2.

CHAPTER VII

A Vicissitude of Civilization

★

Society is always sick, but it is not always mortally sick. The great reversal of our time—namely the displacement of liberal outlooks by collectivist ones, of capitalist economies by socialist ones, the emphasis upon order at the expense of freedom—goes on with varying intensities and methods. Behind it all is another phenomenon which is not part of the economic and political movements involved, but which constitutes the background process in which they operate. It is the phenomenon of a civilization at a particular phase in its career—and I have no hesitation in saying in a downward phase of its cycle. By that I do not mean that everything in it is in dissolution.

I have said that society is always sick. It is always sick because it is never free from destructive forces, such as division in human aims or discrepancies between central policies and personal goals; there are anglings for power and plain human sin. But society has at the same time its own recuperative impulses and powers; there is a self-healing principle which tends to bend policies, theories, conflicts and behaviour, so as to serve the needs of human existence. Therefore, the state of society is not to be judged merely by looking at either the forces of destruction or the forces of healing in it. We must consider the extent and rate of the two processes in comparison. Are the forces of growth or of decline gaining the upper hand? If the question in this form were kept in mind, many obscurities and a good many misleading remedies would be avoided. It would save us from the false progressivism which looks only at the forces of growth and imagines them to be decisive; it would save

A Vicissitude of Civilization

us, too, from the spurious conservatism which is sensitive only to the disintegrating factors and hankers after a return to the day before yesterday when the rot had not gone so far, mistaking it for a period which built upon the permanent constitution of man.

What is the civilization we are talking about? What is its span? We could take a very long span and consider the whole cycle of Western culture from the Greeks; or the unique character of European society formed by the Christian world view. But let us speak of modern civilization, as Toynbee calls it, from the fifteenth century to our own day. I have already in these lectures posed the question whether the reactions to free-market economy which is the *apogee* (the point furthest from the earth) of the liberal, rational and utilitarian outlooks—whether these reactions are merely reversing the trends of this modern period, or whether they cut so deep that the world is returning to a pre-Christian, pre-classical, pre-rational state of affairs. I have had my say about this question elsewhere.[1] Here we have to confine ourselves to the more immediate factors accompanying the decline of capitalist economy.

First of all, to see the issue between capitalism and socialism against the background of a civilization which has passed its peak will prevent a certain amount of mud-slinging at one's opponents in this dispute—though that may not be regarded as an advantage from the point of view of political polemics. If the high hopes of an epoch are becoming a disappointment then backward-looking men will be blaming the innovators for making this worse, quite unjustly, for the decline was happening anyway—and the new seekers, able only to plan within the declining culture, will attribute their poor success to the reactionary forces which resist change. If two sets of people are sliding down a slope at different speeds, it may be a slight advantage to be the one behind; you never know what might come to the rescue before you reach the Gadarene cliff—but to be behind is not to find an upward turn. Nor, of course, is it any real reversal of the perilous descent to make the foremost group into a closer collectivity.

To get away from this ridiculous 'slope' metaphor, defenders and opponents of capitalism—or of socialism—will be blaming the other party for a worsening of the human lot and a weakening

A Vicissitude of Civilization

of human resolve, conditions which are due to the creative impulse of this particular civilization being in process of extinction. Neither party can revive this nor see the need for reviving it, for they both believe that it belongs to man by nature or progress.

There is not much difficulty, either, in detecting how much similarity there is of belief in the characteristics of a particular civilization in those who fight hardest about the way it is to be run. Marx himself, and in our day Berdyaev and Peter Drucker, have emphasized how the cultural aims of capitalism and socialism are largely the same. You will find it written in Drucker's *The End of Economic Man*, under the heading 'The Failure of the Churches': 'The history of the hundred years before the world war is usually seen as the history of the growth and development of bourgeois Capitalism and of its Siamese twin and antagonist, Marxist Socialism. Yet it can be also interpreted as the history of the emergence of Christian criticism of the mechanical and economic concept of society.' His criticism is that 'the Churches' have nevertheless been unable to formulate a new constructive concept of society—in correction of economic and then political man.

Sidney and Beatrice Webb did hope to see the problem in terms of civilization, witness the title of their two works, *The Decay of Capitalist Civilization* and *Soviet Communism: A New Civilization*. In the first of these works, which I incline to think is the best they wrote, the Webbs spoke of the hypertrophy (unhealthy overdevelopment) of the market organization—salesmanship—and attributed this to capitalist motives of profit. It now transpires that the same disease has to be endured not for profit, but for continued employment in an economy less responsive to real demand as it becomes more industrial and mechanized. In the second of these books they were misled by not appreciating that Soviet communism is only new in the sense that it differs from Western society in grafting Western technical and economic methods on to a relatively tribal and non-political society. The superstructure rides on a solid basis of clannish mass community.

I have said as a broad generalization that the Great Reversal is marked by a substitution of the state principle for the economic

A Vicissitude of Civilization

principle—but we have also seen that the state principle is filled out with loyalties that arise out of the pre-political realm, the nation, racial solidarity, the English way of life, French humanism, the Slav soul, American pioneer spirit and so on. The point to be emphasized here is that the state principle and the economic principle—although in a certain antagonism to one another—are both on one side of a line—on the other being the pre-political and pre-economic layers of existence. Ortega y Gasset says: 'The State begins when man tries to escape from the natural society of which he has been made a member by blood. And when we say blood we might also say any other natural principle, language for example. In its origin the State consists of the mixture of races and of tongues. ... Thus the city springs from the reunion of diverse peoples. On the heterogeneous basis of biology it imposes the abstract homogeneous structure of jurisprudence. ... In the genesis of any state we see or guess at the figure of a great "company promoter".'[2]

We have dealt in earlier lectures with the effect of abstracting the economic gain motive from the concrete settings of men in the elements of 'clan' organization which survived the rise of the state. The problem is not one of *state* principle versus *economic* principle, but of state or economic motives in a bid to possess the uprooted mass of men. That is what I mean by state and economic principles being on the same side of the line—the line that separates rational, activist, individualized, civilized man from the organic, tribal and neighbourhood elements which precede and also underlie his more sophisticated constructions. One of our themes has been that the hypertrophied development of economic man has undermined the 'gentile' foundation of all society. The substitution of the state principle does not by itself restore it—though it could perhaps do so with proper awareness and a supreme abnegation on the part of new political masters.

Considerable insight into this dependence of the 'activist' principles of the Enlightenment upon the more rhythmic past was shown by Walter Bagehot. 'In 1789', he wrote in *Physics and Politics*: 'when the great men of the Constituent Assembly looked on the long past, they hardly saw anything in it which could be praised, or admired or imitated; all seemed a blunder—a complex

A Vicissitude of Civilization

error to be got rid of as soon as might be. But that error had made themselves. On their very physical organization the hereditary mark of old times was fixed; their brains were hardened and their nerves were steadied by the transmitted results of tedious usages. The ages of monotony had their use, for they trained men for ages when they need not be monotonous.'

It is the same point, men cannot be on the stretch all the time—and if the 'cake of custom' grows thin, the spirit of man wilts under the burden of incessant adaptation and activity. Civilization is a superstructure; it must stand on a more elemental foundation than itself if it is to survive.

Now it would be fantastic, romantic and theologically false, to say that the urge which builds civilization upon those more elemental layers of human life is a mistake. On the contrary, it is an urge which belongs to man's *natura*, only it can become the enemy instead of the charioteer of the natural powers. Without a religion which bends the spirit of man to God who is ground of Nature and of created spirit, spirit will become the destroyer of Nature. Let us look at this human propensity in terms of the spirit of man—which in Christian terminology is that part of him made in the *image of God* (formally, not morally). Civilization is not natural to man. He does not everywhere develop that particular impress of his creative powers upon the external pattern of life which activity we can take as a provisional definition of civilization. Until véry recent times civilizations, with their ups and downs, were confined to certain definite blocks of the human race, and many groups of mankind remained in a condition of tribal organization, of food gathering, and worshipped none but local deities. The birth of civilization seems to have been marked by a transcending of these limits, by general ideas of a life worth living beyond those necessary for tribal survival, by agriculture and its sequels in definite economic production, and by the worship of high gods. Ethics, conquest of Nature and some view of the nature of ultimate reality which correlates phenomena because it transcends them, are the three main components of civilization. The way they interact determines the form of particular civilizations.

The civilizing impulse in mankind is then an historic pheno-

A Vicissitude of Civilization

menon which arises under certain conditions. It is one activity of the spirit of man. Spirit belongs to man by his particular nature, but it creates civilization only under certain historic conditions. Put theologically, man has spirit by creation; he begins to make civilization when his spirit is confronted by a particular kind of historic situation in the divine dispensation. The civilizing impulse is contagious; civilizations have spread, they have not evolved. Moreover, the advent of civilization is also the beginning of history.

History means that man has learnt to stand somewhat out of the mere succession of generations; he can then trace a connection in the succession and make a pattern of living which is meant to last and to which the succession of generations is meant to minister. Civilization is then one of the attempts to express on earth his superiority to mere natural process. History is the story of those attempts, the story of the impress of his spirit upon process. It has often been noted that the Bible begins with a garden and closes with a city. The Christian drama of human destiny therefore insists that the character of the *Civitas* is in some ultimate sense an integral part of man's essence and fulfilment. Civilization derives from that element in man by which he stands beyond Nature and history. He makes civilization because, though he is involved in them, he is not entirely a product of Nature and history. Civilization-making is that activity in which man seeks to fashion a home for himself, spirit and body, in the natural and temporal context to which he belongs as a creature; a moulding of things and process to reflect as far as may be the needs of his spirit. It is an extension in space and time of man's participation in the transcendent absolute reality, an extension which has its first instalment in human language. Civilization is the man-made surrogate for the Kingdom of God.

This relation of civilization and the spirit of man has a double aspect, which makes civilization both the glory and the tragedy of man. In the first place, civilized living, being a form imposed by man upon the external organization and direction of his existence, releases energies for activities which are not directly practical; the technical and moral activities of civilization give rise to the cultural—the arts and sciences. Moreover, when these activities form

A Vicissitude of Civilization

a tradition in thought and practice they provide individual men with resources beyond their personal contributions. Civilization has a certain life of its own on which men can count to carry them over the patches at which their powers are not at their best. It serves as a home for man in his temporal pilgrimage. But this supporting of man by civilization only operates when it is flourishing —that is, when it embodies the creative powers of the epoch to which it belongs. When it decays, man is lost; he becomes a 'hobo' without a home; he feels dragged along with a culture that has lost its life. He tries to compensate for this loss of vitality by greater external organization and frantic appeals to himself and his fellows for loyalty to a pattern of life which no longer appeals by its intrinsic excellence. This is one aspect of what Emil Brunner calls the demonic character of civilization;[3] it lies in the double aspect of civilization by which it is at the same time the product of man's spirit and the asphyxiator of that spirit.

This is to say that while man's freedom and power brings about civilization, the civilized structure after a time becomes part of his environment and therefore constitutes an element of determinism in his life. Then it may be a temptation to him. It will be asked: How can civilization be a temptation to men? Isn't it just the organized way men want to live? And isn't the life of a civilization one of the highest human achievements? It cannot, you will say, be a snare to people, though they may be lured by their own perversity to destroy it. We have now to see that in certain periods the current organization of life is a temptation and that is a danger for civilization itself. It is a concern for all of us now, because while we of the Western world value the civilization we share, we have an uneasy suspicion that it may not be there for our children's children. Don't we all, to our dismay, really know that this Western civilization no longer exercises the leadership in the world which it once did; and that men do not readily give up their occupations and lives to protect it from enemies; and haven't we in some way lost faith in it ourselves? It is not so much that it is threatened from without, as that it is weakened from inside, and then powers outside move in to exploit the situation.

I am sure that many who still believe that our Western society,

A Vicissitude of Civilization

with its sources in classical times, in the Christian tradition and in what is called the liberal culture, is in some ways the fullest expression of human nature—also feel that there have been forces within it so corrupting that we are in a state of double-mindedness and hesitancy about its future. It may help to dispel some of that hesitancy to realize what we considered more fully in Chapter 3, that civilization is not the same as the aims of man in it; sometimes it menaces the best aims people have. But, when you have seen this, though your minds may be a little clearer, it won't relieve this or any generation from the need for resolute and hard choices. Many are now ready for such desperate decisions but they don't know which way to direct them. Those hard choices may not be spectacular heroisms, but alteration of habits which have become almost second nature in this particular civilization.

We considered that the pattern of a civilization is made up of two parts: the things most people and their leaders want to have done, their aims—and secondly, a large number of forces and tendencies which are not 'willed' but are in the momentum of the civilization. So, when men of the nineteenth century set about increasing wealth, they did not 'will' such results as the shrinking markets or unemployment or the restrictive controls that followed. The pioneers who carried over the world, say, British political ideas and cultural institutions did not 'will' the economic exploitation which often accompanied that process. Also, those engaged in the commercial and technical enterprise on a large scale did not 'will' the threat it has become to free institutions and to the religious and intellectual inheritance which had for so long directed our Western society. Nevertheless, these things happened. That is what I mean by the 'unwilled' forces in a civilization. Men fought in the last war in the name of certain things we believed in, like the rights of persons, equality before the law, the four freedoms and so on, and then we found that these things were endangered not from outside alone but by the drift of things at home.

To renew a weakening civilization requires mainly that its leadership recognize first of all the importance of these 'unwilled' forces and then set about dealing with them—changing them if they are found to be in conflict with the best aims men have.

A Vicissitude of Civilization

Otherwise two things will happen. One is that our advisers go about saying peevishly that the aims of men aren't good enough. Or else, men become rebels against even the good aims of society and go over in their loyalty to an alien and inhuman programme, persuaded that it is in the real human interest.

My main point is that civilization becomes a temptation when people take all of it for granted as certainly of value to human beings. This becomes very serious when we have no standards from outside our civilization by which to judge which of its forces are helpful and which are detrimental.

Civilizations have grown up through men striving for something else, and this has formed a pattern of social structures and habits of life. Ancient Egypt, for instance, produced one kind of culture by concern with the physical immortality of its kings; the Romans by a certain horse-sense in seeking to govern a vast area with diverse cultures; the medieval world in learning to praise God by making all activities, from government to buying and selling, into vocations; the modern world, which is ours, has grown a kind of civilization by man seeking to master the physical world and to understand himself by natural reason. Civilizations—like happiness —come as by-products of pursuing human aims. That is why the sources of civilization are outside itself.

Then again, as elaborated earlier, a civilization rests upon real groupings and associations which are not created by it, such as families, churches, work associations, play teams or local neighbourliness—and especially upon religious and ethical convictions. Men have turned to these more elemental realities when their civilization seemed to fail them; not as escapes, but as sources of strength with which they could go through disorder and disaster without losing nerve, and sometimes sow the seeds of future renewal. But when these elemental foundations have been weakened or destroyed, and when people place all their faith and hope in the civilization—then when it begins to wilt, they have nothing to turn to. So they fall into apathy or resentment, and neither of these is of any help for rebuilding society.

Albert Schweitzer, one of the greatest figures of our time—distinguished as a theologian, as a musician and as a medical mission-

A Vicissitude of Civilization

ary in Equatorial Africa, wrote a book on *The Decay and Restoration of Civilization*.[4] There he said that a civilization depends upon two things besides its conquest of the physical world. These two extra things are a view of the universe, that is its religion or philosophy of the nature of existence, and its ethics, that is its convictions of certain human obligations which stand above what is conformable to this or that civilization.

Now I only want to point out this. If men think that only their 'willed' aims form civilization, and if they have no other loyalties by which to judge what is going on—then they will take all their beliefs from their civilization itself. If part of what is going on is wrong, men will not know it is going wrong or how. On an earlier page I have called attention to a common experience that should help us to understand the frequent conflict between the kind of life we want to lead and our actual behaviour. Each of us has often decided to act in a certain way—say to be considerate to a tiresome person—and then at the critical moment we act entirely contrary to our resolution. It means that some forces in us have overridden our 'willed' aim. In a New Testament parable one son said he would not go to work in his father's vineyard, but he went. The other son said he would, but he did not act on his intention. And we saw how St. Paul gives the religious account of that situation: 'The good that I would I do not, and the evil that I would not that I do.' You can find the same problem stated in the eighth book of St. Augustine's *Confessions*. Another power is at war with the man's good aims. St. Paul finds these two parts of his life reconciled only when he has submitted to the grace of God. When you and I say 'I was not myself', we are distinguishing between the self that means well and that part of us which has not backed up our aim—and has in fact overcome it.

If you now transfer this insight to the question of civilization, then you can disentangle two similar things: the ideals men hold in it, the things they want to do and be; and then the momentum of the civilized set-up itself which has often a direction of its own. When a civilization is on its upswing, the two forces back each other up; when it is declining the aims of men may still be high ones, but the 'unwilled' forces are pulling the other way. Schweitzer, whom

A Vicissitude of Civilization

I have quoted, believes that in our modern world they began pulling the other way after the eighteenth century. Be that as it may, there is a strong temptation to attend only to the dominant aims of a society, for they give men their pride of life, and not to examine the drift of the civilization. We've got so used to the drift —we float along on it—that we take it as natural, and do not easily see that our difficulties lie there.

There are some personal analogies to this situation. Here are two from the sphere of personal relations and work. I knew a man who suddenly lost his ability to do good writing when his marriage broke up. And I was told of two young scientific workers who failed to make any further discoveries when they moved from their native town with poor equipment to a much more favourable environment. Here were men who did not suspect that their aims could only be reached in certain situations which did not look as if they had anything to do with their purposes.

With regard to our own modern Western civilization, in the nineteenth century our society tried to combine two things—or rather thought they were two parts of the same thing. These were, on the one hand our political and cultural ideas and institutions, bound up with the liberties men valued—and on the other hand the development of industrial powers and large-scale organization and world trade, with their sequels in the mechanization of society. This second set of forces became more and more automatic, so that now you cannot call a halt even when some of them seem harmful; they have become a kind of second nature. It was not obvious that this process was in many ways in opposition to the first set of aims—those aims that sought, at home and abroad, to extend opportunities to more people for the kind of life Western civilization had taught men to value. It was believed that you could add the new technical powers and organization to the old ethics and culture and politics, and it now appears that the ethics and culture and politics have turned into something quite different. It has often been seriously asked, for instance, whether a democratic and libertarian society can indeed exist when the political and economic units are beyond a certain size. In other words, if you want certain aims to be achieved you may have

A Vicissitude of Civilization

to question a lot of other things you have taken for granted as irrelevant, inevitable or even beneficial.

Civilizations in the past have got their principles of judgement from their religions or some ultimate convictions about reality which have a religious force. When Christianity helped to form Western society it related things to the reality of the Kingdom of Heaven and to a world view in terms of creation, fall, incarnation, death and resurrection. This was not thought to be achieved or embodied in any historic order, but from insight into it men could mould the world into a certain pattern that in part reflected it, and could recognize sharply when it was a tragic failure. There was a kind of alternative culture, that of the Church, which provided resources of power and criticism and repentance for what men did in the world. Our modern civilization still tries to live by the moral and human goals handed down from an earlier period. These aims are often defeated not only by the sins and faithlessness of men, for that is always the case, but also by the tendencies of a civilization built upon an entirely different world view. The temptation of our civilization is to regard these aims and values as always with men, whereas in fact we have them as a heritage. And that heritage held not only these aims but convictions about the nature of things, and it provided men with a pattern of ritual and conduct side by side with life in the world. But a civilization cannot hold on to these aims for long without the rest of the religious culture they grow out of. For as it says in the Gospel: Do men gather grapes of thorns or figs of thistles?

Civilization thus comes under the general paradox of man's existence which Christianity identifies in the doctrines of man as an image of God and of man as a sinner, the creature who because he is a spiritual creature tends to deny his creaturehood. This question of civilization and its ambivalent character is close to the paradox of man as limited creature and as spirit-centred creature, and to the tragedy of assuming his spirit centredness to make him almighty—even over himself. So there has been a tearing away of this spiritual power to make society and history, from its roots in the non-rational context of life, that is, in the most creaturely aspect of social living. Erich Fromm wrote: 'The growing process

A Vicissitude of Civilization

of the emergence of the individual from his original ties, a process which we may call individuation, seems to have reached its peak in modern history.'[5] And Emile Durkheim spoke of the unrest which comes on people when at some layer they do not feel at home in society; no *status*—only what they can earn—will serve them. Part of that is proletarianization. Durkheim called this unrest *anomie*, corresponding to the 'separation anxiety' of infants fearing abandonment.[6] And Paul Tillich makes theology out of the fact that 'Our life has this tension between dependence on the Origin that has produced us and the independence of it through individuality and freedom'.[7]

The problem of civilization is the problem of a being who has this persisting duality—Nature and spirit—doubled within himself, in his unity. Our crisis is largely that one aspect of man's spiritual nature—activistic rationality—being mistaken for the spiritual centre, has led to a demand for revenge by society and Nature in us, and this takes terrible forms—demonic, as Tillich calls them. Bio-centric living supplants logo-centric living when the latter claims too much.

Capitalism was at once the expression of and the sponsor of activistic rationalism in society; first by abstracting the economic impulse from others, and rationalizing away all non-economic bonds and loyalties, not only kings and popes, but fatherlands, families, sex distinctions, national growths, cults and so on; secondly by replacing the religious, the ascetic and heroic virtues by the calculating, commercial and prudential virtues. But the enterprising impulses that led to the second lot of dispositions were engendered by the first lot and gradually lost their force in isolation.

And here is another expert, Eduard Heimann, showing this economic rationality carried over from capitalism to socialism: 'Socialism thus started as an almost literal translation of individualism into the new technical conditions: it serves the same libertarian goal as does individualism, it presupposes the same rational type of man. It only drives the rationalization of institutions beyond the stage attained under individualism. . . . The atomization of the individual and the mechanization of society by technical reason

A Vicissitude of Civilization

are not cured; they are affirmed. What the merger of the socialist principle with that of efficiency does achieve is the creation of a new type of man, who finds the meaning and fulfilment of his life in the enthusiastic participation in the great adventure of communal industrial building, no matter what vicissitudes of personal life this may bring with it.'[8]

Thus socialism may or may not free man from being the slave of his techniques. For as Tillich has said: 'Technical reason subjected man to the blind and cruel laws of a "second nature" completely alien to him and far more impenetrable than the laws of nature itself proved to be in the age of science.'[9]

This 'second nature' of which Tillich speaks is one that inhibits the creative power of renewal. Here are a few examples of the way man to-day is caught in a net which his rational spirit has woven. The development of commercial industrial civilization presupposed a fluid movement across boundaries—a world division of labour. But the real capital which capitalism produced is not mobile; only its financial symbols are. R. G. Hawtrey writes: 'In contrast to nomadic peoples, the cultivator commits himself to improvements fixed in a particular place. Without such improvements human life must remain elementary, and little removed from that of animals. And how large a role have these fixtures played in human history! It is they, the cleared and cultivated lands, the houses and other buildings, the means of communication, the multifarious plant necessary for production, including industry and mining, all the permanent and immovable improvements that tie a human community to the locality where it is. They cannot be improvised, but must be built up gradually by generations of patient effort, and the community cannot afford to sacrifice them and start afresh elsewhere. Hence the *territorial* character of sovereignty which permeates our political conceptions.'[10]

This means that when the economic climate changes—habits of consumption—the rise of rival producers—political breakaways—then this complex equipment has to be kept going even at an economic loss. Because man is like the boy who said 'not being a bird I cannot be everywhere at once'—the concrete human beings

A Vicissitude of Civilization

in a highly interconnected society have to endure economic loss to keep a place at all. Much of the economic frustration and mishaps previously attributed to the profit-motive arises equally wherever the mass of men have to seek employment. Mr. Garet Garrett has shown the effect of the machine upon the canalizing of human activity into ever-narrowing and inescapable channels. 'The Law of the Machine is that cheapness is a function of quantity—and when you cannot sell cheaper and cheaper watches in ever greater quantities at home you turn to natives, then when you find that all the best bazaar sites are taken, you have a surplus—and the people who have produced it begin in a competitive manner to sacrifice their standards of living in order to keep the machine going.'[11] This problem is irrespective of capitalist or socialist organization. It is concerned with this feature of civilization by which the equipment set up by human ingenuity at some point acquires a momentum of its own, loses its resilience and narrows the field of freedom. There is a law of diminishing returns—or, if you prefer, an automatic brake principle—in this power of men to make that artificial frame for living which we call civilization. An old, highly mechanized society like our English one, which now needs refreshment from the sources of life rather than more power and equipment, benefits less than a land like Russia, or China, from each scientific contribution that lengthens man's arm. It may even find its clinical temperature going up.

I have suggested that the problem of civilization has its roots in the paradox of man, as Christian doctrine understands it. To see it thus should preserve us from two errors: the progressive and the romantic. Both these adopt the logical attitude of formal mind; either men's technical propensities have served well, therefore let us have as much of their results as possible; or, this performance is clogging human life, let us get back to Nature.

Such formal mind says, for example, division of labour has enriched and variegated the means of life, therefore the more of it the better; so let us regard the world as one economic field and have a maximum of specialized products and movements of trade. It ignores that specialization is only an enrichment when it brings a welcome addition to an area which is socially and economically

A Vicissitude of Civilization

sound both in its own economy and its way of life. When these are endangered by specialization, the logic of formal mind becomes a menace. Wisdom then consists in building up equilibrium in the parts.

Such formal mind says the use of machinery and applied science has served to raise the standard of millions, therefore it will go on doing so. It ignores that this is true only in so far as it has underneath it an agricultural, domestic, cultural and spiritual life which supports man while he is making use of technical equipment. When it encroaches upon and devastates these it cuts off the bough on which it is sitting.

Such formal mind says every social and political problem is becoming a world problem, therefore there is no use beginning to tackle it in bits here or there. It ignores that man's social and political consciousness is a small-scale affair and can only be enlarged when it is strong where it is. It ignores that this demand for a world outlook makes demands upon the human being which he finds many difficulties in responding to on even a national or civic scale.

Such formal mind says the irremediable destruction of modern technical warfare is only the development of the bow and arrow replacing the hand club. You must accept it—so we are reminded with technical-school logic—as the victim of the first gun had to accept the new weapon with its ungentlemanly advantage. 'There's no stopping progress; and if you want to prevent the utter devastation of the human race you must stop war at any price.' Formal mind presents the human race with the intolerable dilemma: either total absence of war or any means are legitimate. That is to say, no people may try to stop a Hitler, or fight for justice or independence without the guilt of starting a world disaster.

Such formal mind says that a technical civilization is so interlocked and brittle that its dangers can only be averted by a great rise in moral and co-operative collective behaviour. It ignores that the very enlargement of the equipment has weakened the stimulus to and the capacity for moral responsibility in the more immediate areas of family, work and region, and even nation, and it ignores that the bigger the social groups involved the harder it is for collective egoisms to be abated by principle.

A Vicissitude of Civilization

Cannot we hope for a fresh kind of leadership than that of formal mind, which takes the drift of things for granted and tries to adjust the human being to it? If we can, we must look for signs of understanding that the triumph of mind in creating this technical civilization has been a triumph of the most far-reaching part of man, namely his thought; and that in the other layers of his being; his dependence on the earth, his social loyalties, his attachment to things, places, and traditions—in these he requires firmness underneath him, on the smaller scale in which these things are real to him.

Every civilization seems to reach the same point at which its government, its organization, its machinery, its knowledge and the sophisticated habits of its people—all these develop at the cost of weakening the common ground of human existence out of which the whole thing has grown. And our modern civilization has been doing this for over a century on a scale and a rate and an efficiency never known before in the history of man. And it has spread over less-civilized regions who have fed it and worked for its money. But there is now little more room for this kind of parasitic expansion, and this is giving rise to the only real class war, that between peasant and industrial communities.

Therefore all outlooks and programmes should be directed towards replenishing the sources out of which civilization grows. There are three main sources to be attended to, and we have named them the vital, the cultural and the religious. The first is the life-giving power of the earth upon whose organic products the most theoretical technician or paper planner depends in order to live. Warnings about danger here have been given loudly enough. The earth upon which we live is being drained of its power to support animal and human life. Its vital reproductive cycle is broken under the spur of technical urban and commercial aggression. An acre or two of forest is destroyed to make one New York newspaper per issue; in our small island cultivable land is covered with bricks and concrete, not even for houses or for military defence—both of which are vital priorities after food—but for an alleged technical progress which exaggerates the misbalance between superstructure and foundations. Western man with his arro-

A Vicissitude of Civilization

gance in manipulating organic nature has treated the earth as he has behaved towards Almighty God; he has lived on it without acknowledging his dependence, he has used the life it gives him to exploit it; and he turns to it, panic-stricken, in emergencies for a quick recovery from calamities. In addition the town ceases to be a place to live in and tends to become the place of work; men escape from it when they can, living in dormitories that bespatter the countryside. Both urban and rural life are prevented from co-operating mentally for the well-being of mankind. 'Not another acre' away from food-growing and other vegetation, except for housing families and for military defence, might well be the motto for restoration of the vital sources of economic life in highly industrial lands.

The second foundation upon which civilization must rest, and which it is at some point in danger of destroying, is the sense of community, which satisfies man's domestic, social and emotional life and gives him an attachment to a locality and a cultural tradition. We have considered this in some detail in these lectures and we need not go over it again, except to say this: As we would be complete wrecks if every function of our bodies, such as our digestions, depended upon correct acts of thought and will, so the conscious achievements of civilization require that, underneath them, community living has a vitality of its own which goes on without too much attention. When it does require a lot of attention and fostering it is a sign that civilization has reached the stage when it loses its inner spirit. It then battens on its foundations and every move to recover solidarity adds to the top-heavy machinery of life.

Besides these two bases upon which civilizations are reared, the biological and the social, which are not themselves part of it, there is a third and it is the deepest of all. At the root of all civilization-building there is a spiritual urge, an insatiability in man which demands something more than self-preservation or happiness or comfort. We have considered that the impulse which makes civilization is a kind of spiritual restlessness seeking to fashion the structure of life that will satisfy the craving. Now, if this impulse moves men without the conviction that it is called out by a reality already there—the reality of God behind as well as in the world

A Vicissitude of Civilization

order—then all these hopes will be given to the civilization itself. As civilization is brittle and liable to break down, men tend to lose their inner nerve when this looks like happening. We may say that one condition of the survival of a civilization is that men shall not believe only in that. Civilization decays when men will not admit the possibility of its death although they may feel in their bones that it is moribund. If they have no other hope or stay when a culture crumbles every move to restore it seems but to hasten the crumbling. When King Alfred translated Boethius's *Consolation of Philosophy* he inserted some thoughts of his own. In one of them he said the world needs three kinds of men: working men, fighting men, and praying men. We may paraphrase that. The work of the world has to be done, planting the potatoes as it were; that is the economic function. Then society needs protection within and without; that is the political function. But it also needs men and organs to remind it that life is more than planting potatoes in order to live, and more than protection from destruction in order to do more work and have more protection. There is an end beyond both; that is the cultural and especially the religious element.

The upshot is that if the insatiableness of man is denied its proper meat in religious faith then it takes the form of just wanting more and more things, and more and more activity to escape the feeling of purposelessness. 'I have no more territorial ambitions,' said Adolf Hitler when he annexed Czechoslovakia. Possibly he was speaking the truth, for we all think the next thing we want will content us and it does not. We chase every fugitive satisfaction because of an emptiness in ourselves. Men only believe in a civilization when it fulfils certain needs in them for the expression of their spiritual nature. It must stand for some excellence beyond itself. If it does not, then men will be expecting it to be something it cannot be, namely the object of supreme loyalty and devotion. That belongs only to God who is above and behind the world process—transcends it, as we say. This gives each part and event a meaning in relation to the Eternal God and not only in relation to the social whole or to the past and future.

With the realization that civilization is one of the greatest products of the human spirit and yet that it fails man and drags him

A Vicissitude of Civilization

down when it is treated as his total purpose, we get a wider perspective on the problem of capitalist society and the socialist reactions to it. It may be that these are but two phases in the same process of civilization which requires renewal in its foundations and can only go from bad to worse if more extensions are added to the building without that. And renewal always comes, and only comes, when there are sufficient people who can be sources of renewal out of a faith that does not depend upon the survival of this or that civilization.

NOTES

1. V. A. Demant, *Theology of Society* (London 1947), chap. II; *What is Happening to Us* (London 1949); *Our Culture* (Ed., London 1947), chap. I and VI.
2. Ortega y Gasset, *The Revolt of the Masses* (London 1932), p. 167.
3. Emil Brunner, *The Divine Imperative* (London 1937), p. 392.
4. Albert Schweitzer, *The Philosophy of Civilization*, Pt. I (London 1932).
5. Erich Fromm, *The Fear of Freedom* (London 1942), p. 19.
6. Durkheim's account of 'anomie' is used with great acuteness by Sebastian de Grazia in *The Political Community* (Chicago 1949).
7. Paul Tillich, *The Interpretation of History* (New York 1936), p. 206, chapter on 'The Two Roots of Political Thinking'.
8. Eduard Heimann, 'Rationalism, Christianity and Democracy', a paper in *Festgabe für Alfred Weber* (1948), pp. 165, 166.
9. P. Tillich, 'The World Situation', in *The Christian Answer* (New York 1945).
10. R. G. Hawtrey, *The Economic Problem* (London 1933).
11. Garet Garrett, *A Time is Born* (Oxford 1945), p. 71.

CHAPTER VIII

God's Will and Our Modern Age

★

Christian believers in every age have to ask with proper humility: 'What is God saying to us in this situation?' and that question leads to a more general one: 'What can we trace of God's hand in the events of our time?' It would ill become me to claim to know clearly what God is doing and wants to teach us in the critical transitions of our period. The riddle of history is too dark for that kind of cocksureness. I am as much a child of my own age as anybody else and I am involved in its perplexities—and we have reviewed enough examples which show that men of a certain period assume that they have discovered and corrected the errors and bias and conditioned thinking of previous ages. Christian faith does not free us from perplexities: it does enable us to live with a lot of unsolved problems. That is Christian hope. St. Paul, who said, 'by hope we were saved', also wrote: 'We are perplexed but not in despair.'

Such an attitude leads us to understand God's will as twofold. There is what we may call His ultimate will for the eternal and temporal good of man; but there is also the proximate or relative will of God, declared to this man or this age, for the best to be done just because men do not know or do His ultimate will. The law is an example of that, as St. Paul brings out again and again. While God's ultimate will is that men should live by love, while there is sin the law is God's will for the preservation of life and a relative justice in a sinful world. Take an analogy. Physical health and strength is in an ultimate sense the will of God for all men; but when health fails there is a specific will of His for the cure of sickness or a crutch for a cripple. Of course, sometimes a man can find his spiritual fulfilment in sickness which he entirely missed in normal health. Now when civilization is in a rocky condition current programmes for improvement are specifics of this kind; they may or may not lead to recovery, but they are not of themselves the principle of health. Therefore we shall not hear God's word correctly if we identify this or that system with the ultimate will of God. But we should also be failing to respond to His call to us if we did not commit ourselves to a programme we honestly believed to make the lot of men more tolerable. Though the programme has many blemishes, such a commitment is a necessary part of obedience to the divine will; at the same time we have to remember that it is under judgement in the light of God's ultimate will, so far as we can discern it. And there is one more thing. God acts in judgement by not preventing men's actions from working out their inner logic, for that would crush the freedom of man's spirit in which he was created. You will notice how in the Old Testament the Assyrians are spoken of as instruments of Jehovah's judgement upon His chosen people; and in the New Testament the slayers of Christ have in a tragic sense also His warrant and permission. These powers are not good powers, but they are used as ministers of judgement and redemption. As Professor Butterfield puts it, God's terrible non-intervention is His judgement. But look at this sombre fact in another light; the other side of the same truth is this, in the language of Kierkegaard, the century-old Danish writer: 'One man cannot make another man quite free, because the one who has the power is imprisoned in it and consequently has a false relation to him whom he wishes to free. That is why there is a finite self-love in all finite power (talent and so forth). Omnipotence only can take itself back while giving, and this relationship is nothing else but the independence of the recipient, God's omnipotence is therefore His Goodness. For goodness means to give absolutely, yet in such a way that by taking oneself back one makes the recipient independent.'[1] Such is the theological understanding by which Christians may try modestly to see how God works in a particular phase of history: it turns on the double truth that man's life, along with all creation, is in absolute dependence

God's Will and Our Modern Age

upon God as the ground of its being or existence, and that all creatures have an essence or nature independent of Him, and spirit-centred creatures have in addition a freedom still more independent. Through the fact of existence being rooted in God, His operation never ceases to act in it; when man responds to it, that fact becomes known as the way, the truth and the life; when man lives in self-dependence or rebellion, it still acts, but then it is known in wrath, in judgement and anxiety.

With this insight let us review the main considerations which we have drawn from our study of this modern phase of social history, the transition from a free-market economy to one subordinated to centralized political and social demands. I must first take this occasion to defend my title against some criticisms which were bound to arise. I will take only two. I am reminded that in the strict sense capitalism is a neutral term, like gravity, and means only accumulation of productive resources by refraining from using them all up as they become available. Therefore, the critic says, all civilization is capitalist. Of course, the primitive agriculturalist who keeps back some seed for the next sowing instead of eating it all is a capitalist: so is the plant itself; and a socialist economy with vast fixed assets for future production is also capitalist in that sense. Again, I have been called to task for suggesting that capitalism is a modern phenomenon, whereas financial and economic exploitation are old features of history and whereas money-lending, usury and the power of wealth can be traced long before the sixteenth century. True again, and my first lecture pointed it out. But the thing we have been looking at—the thing which is generally known as capitalism—is a much newer and short-lived event, namely the phase in which social and economic relations became determined almost entirely by free play of the market in the buying and selling of things, labour and services. Both in the small-scale, relatively individualist and domestic business phase and the later monopolistic phase, capitalism, in the historic sense which these lectures presumed, means that state in which not only the products, but also the elements of society—especially its resources in men with their labour, in the land on which society stands and by which it is fed, and in the financial symbols of its fixed plant, namely its liquid capital—the place and function of these elements become themselves determined by the interplay of market and price values. It never entirely covered the whole field, or it could never have gone on so long; but it cut sufficiently deep to make the productive success it was result in colossal social dislocations. We traced its decline to four main causes: the hostility it brought on itself, the break-up of its own institutional framework and defeats of its demands for indefinite expansion, its parasitism on the non-economic foundations of society, and destruction of the dispositions which impelled it.

Now, this has taken place in a phase of Western culture which is largely that of Christendom. And we have tried to unravel the significance of that fact. In doing so we came to a curious discovery which is quite baffling to all who want their history entirely in terms of the good and bad. It is that certain features of modern Western civilization which are contrary to a Christian view of things and its estimate of man, are nevertheless outgrowths of something Christianity made possible. This suggests that Christianity is a very dangerous religion; for when its faith fails to inform the culture it so largely induced, man is in a more risky predicament than if he had remained pagan.

We can look at this a little more in detail, but you will find its background drawn out in the works of Mr. Christopher Dawson, who in his latest work *Religion and the Rise of Western Culture* explains how it came about that 'a small group of peoples in Western Europe should in a relatively short space of time acquire the power to transform the world and to emancipate themselves from man's age-long dependence on the forces of nature'.[2] To summarize some previous arguments, let us review four features of Western culture which have roots in an outlook formed by Christianity and the Bible. That outlook served to give a terrific impress to the discovery of the self, or soul—relating it to the eternal God as well as to its setting in the world; it emancipated man not only in his mind as the Greek had done, but in the depths of his being, from being merely a part of the tribal or social or natural process. At the same time it trained this emancipated being by the belief and rituals and ethics and law of Christendom. It is this discipline that

God's Will and Our Modern Age

has faded out in the modern world while the sense of standing over the cosmic process remains.

In the second place, only in Christendom did you get that division of life into sacred and secular, due to the doctrine of creation and then to the separation of religious and civic leaderships. Christianity was never identified with one particular political or cultural historic growth but overarched a great many different ones. Then it presented man with the problem within these christianized communities of adjusting the two loyalties, to the things of God and the things of Caesar, or to the spiritual and the temporal order, for both are of God in different modes. The point is that by the very nature of the Christian religion there came into being a 'secular' realm which had its own responsibility to God, and not directly through the Church. A large part of Christian theology deals with the relation and distinctness of these two realms of obedience; and much European history is about the tension between them. The term 'secular' had a Christian origin, meaning that which belongs to 'this age' between creation and the last day, in contrast to the eternal realm where one day is as a thousand years and a thousand years as one day. In recent times the religious setting of all this has broken up and we have this secular sphere owning no other reality beside itself. That is what we mean by secularism and it is a rebellious child of Christendom.

In the third place, Christianity gave a great stimulus to the sense of history as significant. God in the Old Testament is revealed first of all as the Lord of History. Then the Christian faith, as we have already described, made the relation of each man and each event to the Eternal God a precise relation to the person of Jesus the Christ, in whose flesh the Eternal God enters directly into the temporal and historic scene. He is the second Adam, the republication of the origin of all things; He appears, dies and rises from the dead at what the New Testament calls 'the end of the times'— anticipating the final end when history will be wound up and its meaning fully disclosed. Christian man learnt to see or feel his life as being not only part of the rhythm of Nature, not only an item in the irreversible movement of history, but also in a third dimension of existence, namely that represented by the creation, the incarnation and resurrection of Christ, and the last day, and the Church as a new history beside the old. He is thereby placed in a realm of existence which cuts across the groupings in which He participates as part of the world process, such groupings as His tribe, city, empire, class and associations, and their histories. All this tended to give Western man a consciousness that history was not a mere flux; it could be discerned as a cosmic-spiritual drama. It was a drama enacted in terms of two worlds: the temporal or this age, and the eternal, of which the Epistle to the Hebrews speaks when it describes the Christians as those who have tasted of the powers of the age to come. Man could therefore make history because he stood to some extent outside the mere succession of generations.

When, later, the modern period had heightened this disposition to make history and at the same time rejected the cosmic-spiritual scheme and the divine-human context out of which the disposition had grown—we find the whole of human existence interpreted in terms of the world or the historic process. First, the reason would get the irrational hurdles one by one out of the way of man's completely masterful life. We have seen that the sacred element comes back in the form of holiness given to some development of the secular order. In terrible forms of fanaticism, the secular tends to become demonic.

In the fourth place, there follows from the previous three developments the extraordinary activism of Western man. 'The other great world cultures', writes Dawson, 'realized their own synthesis between religion and life and then maintained their sacred order unchanged for cultures and millennia. But Western Civilization has been the great ferment of change in the world, because the changing of the world became an integral part of its cultural ideal.'[3] This activism has remained and increased, with diminishing respect and reverence towards God and the universe.

These are the ways in which we can trace how things that were born out of Christendom have become a menace when cut off from their religious context. I think we must see the hand of God in warning and judgement acting in two ways: one in not having yet stopped the enterprise of Western man (though there are ominous signs), for that would be winding up the career of Christendom. He who did not exterminate man at the first movement of sin, and who did not stop the crucifixion, does, it seems, out of some inscrutable care for man's independence, allow man's fate to work out as man makes it. The other way in which we may trace His writing on the wall is to notice that the reactions, in the history of our time, to the predicaments of the Western spirit, seem like a blind move to get behind the whole development of individuation and of reason, of secular autonomies and the distinction between Church and society. Those reactions, informed by much of the arrogance of the liberal phase, tend to revert to a pre-Christendom kind of solidarity. We have already named this reaction a pull of man's nature away from one aberration and described it as landing him in another. The only corrective for a continuation of this dangerous spin is to have some guiding principle about the fundamental needs of men and their proper order—priorities, as they say nowadays. This will involve an understanding that man is a spirit-centred creature and that this has a sociological as well as a personal reference. We have seen that this spirit-centredness of man has an ambivalent force—its freedom can destroy his concentric nature or it can recover it. In the personal life the true centrality cannot be sustained by the individual man remaining self-contained, but only by allowing the Divine Action to operate upon and through him, keeping his spiritual centre truly central, and the outer parts of his existence then falling into their proper order. This is the process begun and carried through by the practice of religion. In the same manner, the centrality of the spirit in its sociological reference cannot be sustained by moral desire alone; it requires a social order formed to minister in its priorities to the nature of man. This is to say, human living becomes disordered not only when the human spirit, in stark idolatry, deifies one of its powers, such as the reason, exchange, production, the state, sex or art; but also and equally when, however fine its intentions, it exercises any of these powers on a plane which does not belong to it. The most general layers of human life round the spiritual centre are the cultural, the political and the economic activities. Religion is not included because it is not an attitude of man to one aspect of his life, but a relation to God behind them all, which pulls man round so that these fall into their rightful places and reinforce one another by each performing its proper function. Here is an outline of an order in these general human activities with some indication of the consequences of its violation.[4]

The cultural side of life, its arts, knowledge and ceremonies—all that qualifies life and does not merely preserve it—has a precedence over politics and economic activities. It is a metaphysical and not a physical or moral precedence. Life must be sustained by economic activity, it must be protected and co-ordinated by politics before it can be enriched and adorned. These have a physical priority over the cultural stratum. And, also, the practice of the arts which adorn life, whether aesthetic, scientific or spiritual, is in no sense morally higher than that of government, industry or commerce. Cultural activities have a metaphysical priority in that in them the spirit of man operates most centrally from within outwards, less conditioned by the determinisms which of necessity belong to political and economic activities. Cultural goods grow by the sharing of them, whereas politics is largely the checking of power by power and economics is concerned with the making and distribution of things and the comparison of effort put forward with the satisfactions gained. Cultural bonds are more essentially spiritual and universal than political or economic ones. Therefore a society in which the cultural life has not a certain priority in this sense violates the natural order of man's inner structure. It can be violated in several ways: if provision is not made for people to teach and carry on the religious, educational, aesthetic, and scientific arts; if any class is so exhausted in one of the more practical tasks that it has no opportunity, energy, or guidance for cultural pursuits; if the cultural domain is treated as an adjunct for political consolidation, as this sphere is in totalitarian societies; or if it is prostituted to keep the economic process going, as it largely is in the democracies.

The political functions include government, maintenance of military power, law, and the police, the establishment of a balance of rights and duties. Politics represents the collective effort of the spirit of man to protect life from the threat which resides in the

God's Will and Our Modern Age

egoism of men and groups and to co-ordinate on the basis of certain common values the activities of organized society. In itself the political function is more involved in the determinisms of Nature and history than the cultural, but is nevertheless a form of spiritual mastery over them. It has therefore its own moral responsibility. This is not that of forming the ethical and cultural purposes for men, but of enabling men with diverse non-political purposes to live with that degree of solidarity which a common citizenship requires.

The economic activity is in itself the most tied to physical realities. By it men transform material from the earth and move it about. In developed societies economic activity is much more than spending effort upon material. The organization of production and distribution represents a great impact of the human spirit upon the physical and human realities. Because of this real but limited control of material facts and processes by will and intelligence, the economic sphere is one where the natural order is to-day most violently deranged. This happens in two opposite ways: when man's spiritual control over economic life is in effect denied, and when the limitations upon that control are similarly denied.

The first denial takes place when real political aims are given up or defeated by forms of economic behaviour which are not dictated by the physical and energy basis of economics. For instance, one of the factors in our British failure to oppose aggression was the extent to which the needs of trade were regarded as paramount or mistaken for basic economic needs. Now, when policy assumes that economic satisfactions and economic bonds are supreme in human relations, it is often called to account by men themselves brushing aside rational economic calculations and striving for some political or cultural goal even at the cost of conflict and war. And in moments of great human tension men seek out their cultural compeers in preference to political ones, and political ones in preference to economic ones.

When the cultural and political aims of men are not given their essential priority over economic purposes in the organization and habitual attitudes of society, economic means and ends become reversed. Now, for instance, employment is treated as an economic and even as a political aim; whereas it is a necessary expenditure of effort, varying according to the skill of the community in drawing energy direct from the earth, so as to supply the physical basis of personal, political, and cultural achievement. And when this treatment of employment as a goal is defended on the moral ground that we cannot have the awful spectacle of the unemployed, it only proves that attempts to satisfy moral requirements, without bothering about other aspects of the natural order, are bound to be ridiculous.

On the other hand, man's technical and organizational handling of the world, which is the work of the spirit, leads him to seek unnatural freedom from the limitations to which economic activity is subject. This provokes colossal conflicts of purposes within economic life itself. While production and distribution are logically secondary to use and enjoyment of things, historically we have in our modern world reached a position where the community is expected to cultivate needs to satisfy the productive and trading agents' need to be kept going. This diversion of means and ends is carried a step further when production is directed by the interests of exchange and both these by the dominant interest of the money-lending power. This all means that the physical *raison d'être* of economic activity becomes subject to highly organized devices of ability in which spiritual control over things and men has become a power in itself, used for gain or for satisfactions, divorced from economic ends.

The primary economic activity is rooted in the region where its material is to be had. This is the natural economic basis of the social and cultural life of that region. The activity of its members can overspill into economic relations with other communities. But if it is more than an overflow that exchanges goods and services between societies relatively whole in their economic balance, there comes about a disintegrating effect upon the community centres themselves. Greater specialization between regions into primary and secondary producers on the one hand, or close links between narrow, strong economic interests across real community boundaries, like heavy industry, commerce, or finance, on the other, tend to destroy the proper hierarchy of social functions in each community. These tendencies also exacerbate international rivalry in spite of the rationalized belief that they will diminish it. World trade is an expression of man's will and intelligence over material limitations—that is the work of the human spirit—but when it proceeds to the point where other factors of his existence which require local growth are despised or the attempt is made to stretch them to fit the economic interdependence, the break-up of community is imminent in every part concerned. Cultural excellence spreads abroad when it has been attained in one region; so very often does political achievement. Economic relations can only be mutually beneficial when they are of the same kind, spreading from healthy centres. This century has witnessed a colossal endeavour to cure economic dislocations within each region by seeking to extend economic relations over wider and wider areas. So our civilization presupposes more and more secondary and trading activity as the main economic function, with food producing and the building up of healthy regions as regrettable menial necessities. This is the result of neglecting both the proper obedience to the organic basis of community life and the fact that men will not work a society where the demands of their psychic, cultural, and political life are maimed for the sake of a delusive rational economic world scheme, even when they do not detect that it has become a vested interest overriding all cultural and political loyalties.

Where the natural order is seriously contravened in any set of relations, the disorder infects all the others. Particularly, each activity which is out of its proper place or disordered within, tends to prey upon the activity above it in the natural scale. Within the economic layer itself the most instrumental part is money. When money becomes the commodity of a vast business in lending and exchange it ceases to be a true distributive mechanism. In consequence trade in goods and services becomes secondary to exchanging and lending money and to the business of credit-creating institutions; then trade calls the tune of the productive enterprise of communities, and the personal consumer becomes a doped and 'propaganded' agent for making production possible, whereas the use and enjoyment which he wants of things should be the purpose of the whole economic process.

God's Will and Our Modern Age

The unnatural order here then draws politics away from its proper function and it becomes a rescue agency for economic collapse. Members of Parliament are expected to 'represent' this or that business interest; success in economic enterprise is supposed to be a qualification for rulership; and a new host of controllers, officials and planners comes into being. This gives a further shove to the tendency which makes for the multiplication of activity as an end to which all economic purposes are subordinate, and the true end of meeting natural human needs is obscured.

In order to avoid the worst effects of economic and political disintegration, education and moral training are then called for, as an aid to the better working of the disordered thing, and the Churches even are expected to provide a spiritual, 'dynamic' social leadership. Education and morals lose their authentic role; religion loses that supernatural basis which has, in the days of the Churches' power, enabled it to speak with authority about the natural order, and it becomes merely the medium of expression for the national soul in its terrestrial moral struggle.

Having considered the meaning of an order of life according to man's essential nature and the deformations of such an order, let us look at the matter in another way. I have interpreted the capitalist period as a remarkable achievement and in the end a calamitous one. That result represents the climax of some logically connected steps beginning with the emancipation of secular spheres from direct tutelage to religion and ethics. In a sense a separation between them was required by Christianity, with the provisos we have considered. The conversion of this separation into a divorce brought about the erection of economic ends to the supreme place among social purposes, and further, the abstraction of the market relationship as the essence of economic reality. Now, it is often said that this has produced a materialistic civilization. I want to examine this because, as it stands, just like that, it is a misleading and over-simplified statement by which people feel they have made a moral and religious judgement. It is true that industrial commercialism in its capitalist phase not only made possible a standard of living for millions which before had only been enjoyed by the more sheltered classes. That is a material benefit no one should resent.

God's Will and Our Modern Age

It is also true, as we have seen, that it also produced some counteracting forces that prevented much further increase in that direction—such as rapid growth of populations in industrial areas, and later the necessity for keeping plant and employment going at some loss, and a financial mechanism with independent aims of its own which in some vital stages birth-controlled a good deal of useful production through failure of distribution. But along with these results and with a commendable rise in living standards in spite of the defeats it encountered—there did grow up a disposition called by the Greeks *pleonexia*, an itch to have more and more, often with no basis in real human needs. Individual and family motives of prestige, snobbery, fear for the future, desire to climb the social scale or more leisure, entered into the picture. And for the advanced economic communities there came a craving for technical *grandeur*, to have the largest airship, for instance, or the power to command cheap labour abroad and become more white-collared at home. The alarming consequence which is felt by those who often complain of materialism, is real enough. It is that the *pleonexia* which was organized and blessed by capitalism has now informed the workers and has invaded the mentality of socialism. To satisfy it, the modern West is using up the resources of the earth much more rapidly than they are reproduced. If the East completely imbibes this spirit from the West the end of Western society will fall at the same time as its influence becomes universal.

But the immediate point is that this *pleonexia*, personal and communal, is to a very large extent not a desire for material benefits, but a spiritual malaise which grows greater with every satisfaction it gets. So that what is called materialist civilization is only in part one which makes greater material gain its object. And if good food, good houses, good clothes and good furniture are objects of the right kind of materialist desire, then our technical society is making a bad job of its materialism. Many a simpler community does these things better.

But when we turn to the origins of the development of capitalist industrial and commercial enterprise, we find that it arises out of a very high development of some of man's spiritual faculties, namely his reason, his science, his politics. These liberated him from the limitations of Nature, of racial, neighbourhood and domestic social groupings, and released energies by freeing him from cosmic and religious fears. All this is a spiritual achievement —the work of the spirit of man in its various activities of extraversion, as it were. This means that modern civilization in its motive force represents a very full development of man's inner forces. This is completely misunderstood when people identify the facts of these inner forces with religion and when they equate the movements of man's spirit with that particular response of it to God which is the movement of religion. What is spiritual is not by itself godly. Incidentally, that is why we are not a whit nearer to genuine religion when we discover, sometimes with the encouragement of scientific thinkers, that the world is ultimately spiritual, though this often means little more than that gross matter is really only a form of energy. An interpretation of existence can be entirely spiritual and at the same time entirely atheistic; it could also be entirely diabolical, for the devil is spiritual. Some light is shed upon this question by George Santayana who, in the volume on 'Religion' in his *The Life of Reason*, says that there are two movements in religion, Piety and Spirituality. 'Piety', he writes, 'is man's reverent attachment to the sources of his being and the steadying of his life by that attachment. . . . This consciousness that the human spirit is derived and responsible that all its functions are heritages and trusts, involves a sentiment of gratitude and duty which we may call piety . . . it contains a much greater wisdom than a half-enlightened and pert intellect can attain.' Spirituality, on the other hand, he describes as the aspiring side of life; it looks to the end towards which we move. 'Though a spiritual man may perfectly well go through intricate processes of thought and attend to very complex affairs, his single eye, fixed on a rational purpose, will simplify morally the natural chaos it looks upon and will remain free. . . . The spiritual man, though not ashamed to be a beggar, is cognisant of what wealth can do and what it cannot.' And then Santayana adds: 'The spirit's foe in man has not been simplicity, but sophistication.'[5] We can say that man is a spirit-centred creature by creation, he has a self-transcending power which no other terrestrial creature has; this power lay relatively dormant until a combination of influences in Christendom turned it into a world-transforming force. Now this self-transcending and masterful power does serve man· but also adds to his perils. The discipline of the Christian life is the submission of this powerful force to the Supreme Spirit. That is the religious form of *pietas*: and it is a pity that this has been obscured by the degeneration of our word piety. Those who have undertaken in any measure to tread the path of Christian inner discipline know that the training of the soul requires as much weaning and purging from spiritual experience, in general, as from vital urges and entanglements with things. The tendency to deify man's own spiritual movements is one of the most subtle and deceptive forms of idolatry. So in the Christian training of the soul the human spirit's self-transcending powers are broken down over and over again precisely in order that the man of faith may know God and not mistake his own spiritual convolutions for the divine action. To repeat a reference, you will find in the second chapter of the First Epistle to the Corinthians how St. Paul marks a clear distinction between the spirit of man and the Spirit of God.

Now, to return to our social diagnosis with this distinction in mind, our economic civilization, which is so often described as materialistic, would more properly be understood as having developed spiritually and having lost the attitude of piety. What modern man and his brittle complicated technical and economic culture most need is to recover some respect for the cosmos. In the thirteenth century, already, St. Bonaventura, in his *Hymn of Creation*, made all created things, the earth, the water, the air, cry out against man: 'This is he who abused us. . . . Why must we bear upon us this monster?—why do we not deprive him of our benefits?'; in our own time Bertrand Russell himself has said that man to-day is guilty of cosmic impiety. There seems to be an inevitable connection between loss of belief in and respect for the deity, and aggressive disrespect for the earth and the conditions it imposes and for the essential structure of human life. This overweening disregard of the laws of life, of which the depredations of the economic age are the outstanding expression, brings its own judgement, and the severest part of that judgement is that the more

God's Will and Our Modern Age

effectively it builds up the equipment of life the more difficult it is to mend the wreckage. A sound society is one which knows what to do when things go wrong; it allows for a proper material and spiritual repair service. Arnold Toynbee calls attention to the way in which the vast paraphernalia of a complicated society, built up by man's spiritual powers, at some point destroys the self-healing principle. He writes: 'A simpler social structure has far greater recuperative powers than a more complicated one. When I see our rebuilding programmes in Great Britain being retarded by shortages of labour and of highly processed materials, and perhaps not least by the mere complication of the administrative machine, my mind goes back to a glimpse that I had in 1923 of a Turkish village reconstructing itself after it had been devastated in the last phase of the Graeco-Turkish war of A.D. 1919-22. Those Turkish villagers were not dependent on materials or labour from outside, they were not at the mercy of red tape. They were rebuilding their houses and replacing their household utensils and agricultural implements with their own hands out of wood and clay within their reach.'[6]

Does this mean that God is bidding us all go and live the simple life? Not at all; though that will be the call he gives to a number of people; and surely leadership in the future will pass to those who are able to understand the world because they have made some withdrawal from it. Shift and expediency to deal with one crisis after another will not make for recovery. We have already come to a general conclusion that it is the extent of the equipment of a highly economic civilization that needs watching, for it tends after a certain point is reached to make for deterioration in the natural, social and spiritual foundations. And we suggested that so long as balance is not restored, men collectively will react in unhealthy and oppressive ways to try to find a life nearer to Nature, to community and to God.

The whole scheme of restoration according to Christianity is built upon the need for that spiritual centre of his to be submitted to the divine ground of existence Who is the principle of unity behind Nature and spirit of man. Then man can become concentric again and all the powers of his fall into their proper order. It

God's Will and Our Modern Age

is when an age tries to find unity within man's own life that one part of it is turned into a dominating oppressor, and he loses the freedom of the spirit—and such freedom is the only source of renewal. The great age of capitalist enterprise worked with a philosophy that ignored this need for repeated and conscious obedience to the laws of being—and this ignorance has been inherited by its socialist successors. We have in this book discussed some problems of men in spheres of contemporary living which are not specifically within the domain of religion. The greater number of those who work and think in them affirm no religious authority for the laws they acknowledge, the standards they work by, and the methods they use. And if they did they would be regarded by many honest men, even outside their own sphere, as playing false to the disinterested search for truth and excellence within it. The examination of the human situation here made has not sought to detract from the proper autonomy which can be claimed for the spheres of life with which it deals, especially the economic, industrial, political and cultural ones. But it has found that there is something of a crisis in the secular spheres themselves, that the proper autonomy of each is threatened. In the economic life of the age of capitalist expansion the aims men pursued were unconsciously accepted as universal, and practical deductions from them were mistaken for permanent human laws. Men tried to read their ethics and philosophy of man out of a particular phase of social history instead of judging that phase with its aims and assumptions by the ethics and total view of human existence. In consequence economic life lost its proper autonomy and became the slave of one of its own activities, namely the market relation; and to-day the total human reality is seeking to redress this aberration by depriving economic life of its freedom which has had such great productive success.

It is all part of a larger tendency. Another movement in the tendency is the fate of Rationalism which exalted the human reason to the very centre of human nature; in consequence it ceased to sustain the right place of reason. In this century we have seen that reason has not remained master even in its own top flat of the human house, and has become the lackey of instinct, feeling, and unconscious urges. The general severing of man, in human thought, from his total context in the religious and natural worlds has left him not magnificently human, autonomously human, but cravenly wriggling under conflicts between the claims of his own means of living, each of which seeks to wrest autonomy from him. The outlook behind the rise of the economic age attempted to give man a status by according him absolute sovereignty in the real world—but it did so by cutting him off from a great deal in the real world—from God, the cosmos, the community, the Church. Because men have links with these things by their essential nature, even when unacknowledged, the severance of them in the world's thought has not only cut round him, it has cut into him. So the human panorama of the last two centuries has presented us not with a pageant of free and kingly lords of creation, but with a succession of ghosts, the economic man, the rational being, the self-expressive artist, a brick in the social edifice, the crown of biological life, or the chosen-race bearer—bits of humanity upon which total philosophies of life have been erected.

In such a succession we see the interaction of two facts, man's freedom to fashion his life and his environment, and a tug from behind that prevents each alienation from his true being from becoming absolute. He is drawn over to a counteracting position, which, though corrective of the first, is still in the sphere of alienation. The Christian thinkers see this situation in terms of God's holding on to man in his being while not crushing the freedom which is his by creation, and allowing it to find its own judgement on its own independent plane.

We have dealt with this swing over and back across a sort of position of equilibrium in its more concealed forms as they affect the different layers of man's social existence. But the most easily seen way in which it operates is the swing from individualism to collectivism. Western culture had given man a deep sense of being a person, a being with roots in an eternal world and operating in this. The liberal humanism of the post-Renaissance age ignored all the social and cultural conditions of this possibility, mainly a certain order in human activities. So the principle of personality came to be interpreted not in the up-and-down dimension of his existence, but in the horizontal dimension as the principle of being a separate unit. Men on the whole were involved in a contradiction they could not detect. They only knew the pains of the result. That pain is what they now call crisis—and it impels them to flee from one form of denying their total nature to its secular opposite. So we have the heresy of individualism swinging round to the heresy of collectivism. The doctrine of absolute collectivity represents the despairing effort of the secularized man to escape from the uprooting effects of the doctrine of the absolute individual. A democracy built not upon the needs of persons to pursue ends for which they are constituted, communal, intellectual, and religious ends, but upon freedom from anything which feels like dependence, had produced an atomization of society which is false to the nature of human existence. This is now being swept into collectivism as an automatic self-correction. But collectivism is but atomism packed tight. Men do not find healed the wound left by tearing them away from their spiritual and organic setting, by collaborating with other men maimed like themselves in a state enterprise or planned economy or racial messianism. The various socialisms of this century have sought to cure the crisis of the individual deprived of community, but have sought it in the horizontal dimension alone. They have inherited from the earlier phase of the economic age the ignorant acquiescence in the disordering of the various spheres of life in the vertical dimension; it was a certain ordering of these that made possible the value attached to the person. The collectivist reaction has not therefore been a response to the call of man's total nature, but only an outbreak from frustrations. And unless renewal takes the form of a response to the ground of all human purposes which constitute man's personality, there is bound to be a surrender to some natural or political or economic absolutism where he loses his individuality without recovering his personality.

The individualism of the last two centuries misinterpreted the significance of the person, regarding it as lying in the over-against relation of one man to others. There was a parallel attitude of standing over-against the world outside and around man, his organic and spiritual setting. It was this attitude, for practical purposes regarding man as a world himself, which prevented the

God's Will and Our Modern Age

age from suspecting that man's power over his environment might perhaps become enfeebled and even destructive of the civilization which sustained those powers and increased them. This irresponsible confidence that men could not undo their civilized achievements had sometimes a religious backing due to misreading of such teaching as is represented, for instance, by St. Paul's phrase about our being 'workers together with God'—as though everything man could do by his ability and organization and overcoming limitations, was, just because it could be done, in line with God's purpose. Our being co-workers with God does not mean that we are His little housemaids and He would be in a terrible predicament if we gave notice. It means that our work must be done His way, that is by the laws of His creation, at His pace, and with His methods. This is a lesson it is much harder for a highly intellectual and spiritually self-conscious age to learn, than for those who live in much closer dependence on Nature. Great religion is, we may say, the discipline by which man, the spiritual creature with these colossal temptations to wreck his life by overmastering independence of the laws of being—great religion is that by which he goes a step further and learns on a new plane to live with the spirit as straightforwardly as he lived with Nature. 'O that my ways were so direct,' cried the psalmist, and it is something of this that Berdyaev, the great European philosopher, had in mind when he wrote: 'A higher degree of spirituality would enable man to commune once more with the mysteries of cosmic life without having to submit to the determinism of its forces.'

There is one final piece of theology I would bring to this question of our age—an age which, in its capitalist and socialist phase, is informed by fundamentally the same outlook that develops man's powers at the cost of wrecking the base from which he operates. The question true leadership should be asking is: does this or that development strengthen man where he is or does it just make more demands on him while undercutting his point of support? This is pre-eminently the question the Christian mind should always be framing, for it thinks in terms of depth and not of extension—where it has not been seduced by a world demanding moral oil for its creaking machinery. Get things more right in the up-and-down dimension—here and now—the dimension in which men are related to God, to their naturally grown communities and to the earth on which they live: then you may hope that the power of recuperation here will extend horizontally and begin the growth of communities as mutually helpful neighbours. Otherwise—we shall join up a lot of bankrupt businesses, hoping that the sum will show a credit balance.

When Pascal, in the *Pensées*, said: 'by means of space the universe encompasses and engulfs me as a pin-point: by means of thought I encompass it', he misled countless people who have fastened on this idea in isolation. They have taken it to mean that by thought all reality could be grasped. But Pascal speaks only of the physical universe, not the whole of human reality. Of this human reality he insisted that it could not be measured by our concepts, or by what we designate the 'possible', but what is possible, as well as our concepts, must be measured by reality.

He brings man back to the contemplation of the universe which is the work of God, and to contemplate man himself—his real needs, power and limitations. Then alone will men not mistake for those realities the artificial constructions which the self-sufficient human spirit without wisdom imagines to be most real.

NOTES

1. Søren Kierkegaard, *Journals* (Oxford 1938), Entry 616.
2. Christopher Dawson, *Religion and the Rise of Western Culture* (London 1950), p. 8.
3. op. cit., p. 10.
4. The following ten paragraphs repeat a section of my essay, 'The Idea of a Natural Order', in *Theology of Society* (London 1947), pp. 86–90.
5. George Santayana, *The Life of Reason*, vol. on Religion.
6. Arnold Toynbee, *Civilization on Trial* (Oxford 1948), p. 134.

Index of Authors

Alfred, King, 175
Aquinas, St. Thomas, 155
Arnold, T., 53
Augustine, St., 73, 145, 166

Bacon, Francis, 66
Bagehot, Walter, 25, 160
Balchin, N., 154
Barnard, C., 153
Bastiat, F., 36
Bellman, H., 84
Belloc, Hilaire, 153
Bentham, J., 52, 66, 79
Berdyaev, N., 58, 135, 151, 156, 159, 196
Bergmann, E., 105, 108, 120, 133
Bevan, E., 84
Boethius, 175
Bonaventura, St., 191
Brentano, L., 18, 33
Bright, J., 25
Brodrick, J., 18
Brunner, E., 163, 176
Buckle, T. H., 130, 133
Bukharin, N., 37, 119 f.
Burnham, James, 21, 33
Butterfield, H., 73, 178

Calvin, 39
Carr, E. H., 28, 34, 75, 135, 155
Church, R. W., 37, 58
Clapham, J. H., 23, 34
Clark, J. M., 136, 155
Cobden, R., 25, 78, 83 f., 130
Cocks, H. F. L., 58
Coleridge, Samuel Taylor, 45 f., 53
Comte, A., 79, 125 ff., 133

Coué, E., 72
Creed, J. M., 113
Cunningham, W., 19, 33

Davies, D. R., 152
Dawson, Christopher, 28, 60, 83, 100, 107, 180, 182, 197
Demant, V. A., 85, 176
Descartes, 77
Dicey, Prof., 80
Dietzgen, 117
Drucker, P., 28, 34, 95, 107, 159
Dühring, E., 120, 133
Durkheim, E., 28, 48, 169, 176

Engels, F., 45, 53, 99, 120 f., 133
Eucken, R., 41

Fanfani, A., 18
Feuerbach, L., 125 ff., 133
Fichte, J. G., 105, 108
Figgis, N., 101, 107
Finer, H., 106, 108
Forsyth, P. T., 133
Frank, W., 131
Frankfort, H., 107
Franklin, Benjamin, 18, 60
Fromm, E., 168, 176

Garrett, Garet, 171, 176
y Gasset, Ortega, 160, 176
Gloyn, C. K., 45, 58
Goethe, 123 f.
Gore, Charles, 15
Gorky, M., 118
de Grazia, S., 176
Greenslade, S. L., 52, 58

Index

Guillian, W. F., 156
Guizot, 60

Halévy, E., 43, 52, 58, 77 f., 84
Hammond, J. L. & B., 43, 52, 58, 82, 140 f., 156
Hardy, T., 130
Hawtrey, R. G., 170, 176
Hayek, F., 104, 106, 108
Hecker, J., 117, 133
Heckscher, E. F., 77, 84
Hegel, 112 f., 122, 126, 133
Heimann, E., 169, 176
Herder, J. G., 46
Hitler, Adolf, 97, 123, 175
Hobbes, T., 139
Holland, H. S., 13 f., 33, 55
Honey, W. B., 125
Hooker, R., 84
Housman, L., 130
Hudson, C. E., 58
Hügel, Baron F. von, 41
Hume, D., 66, 72
Huxley, A., 107
Huxley, T. H., 124, 130

Ibsen, H., 121
Isaiah, 142

James, St., 155
Jaspers, K., 26, 34
Jefferson, T., 79, 96
Jenks, E., 101 f., 108
de Jouvenel, B., 107, 156

Ketteler, W. E. von, 44 f.
Kierkegaard, S., 84, 141, 178, 197
Kingsley, Charles, 14, 117
Klages, L., 123

Lamartine, 60
Lassalle, F., 25, 34
Laski, H., 84
Lattey, C., S.J., 107
Lenin, N., 97, 117 f., 138
Le Play, F., 28, 48, 96
Lewis, C. S., 46
Lindsay, A. D., 39 ff., 58

Lipson, E., 34
Locke, J., 60
Löwe, A., 25, 34, 107
Ludlow, J. M., 54, 58
Luther, Martin, 39, 73

Macaulay, J. B., 130
MacIver, A. M., 34
MacLean, F., 101, 107
Madach, I., 84
Malinowski, B., 85
Malthus, 72
Mandeville, B., 22, 135
Mannheim, K., 38, 48, 59 f., 83 f., 107, 142, 156
Maritain, J., 84
Marx, Karl, 13, 17, 21, 45, 53, 54, 64, 92, 117, 121 f., 124, 126 f., 133, 138, 159
Maurice, F. D., 14, 54
Mayo, E., 28, 34, 140, 153, 156
Mead, M., 85
Meier, B., 108, 156
Mill, J. S., 25, 36 f., 60, 63, 130
Mill, James, 66
Morgenthau, H. J., 34
Morley, John, 20, 33
Morris, W., 50, 125
Mosca, G., 82, 85
Mussolini, B., 105, 108

Nersoyan, T., 133
Newman, J. H., 37
Niebuhr, R., 138, 152, 156
Nietzsche, F., 64, 81, 123 f.

Owen, Robert, 27, 121, 135

Pascal, B., 197
Paul, St., 72, 166, 177, 191, 196
Pirenne, H., 34, 80
Polanyi, K., 23, 34, 58, 80
Prinzhorn, H., 123, 133
Proudhon, 25

de Quincey, 140

Ranke, 113

Index

Raven, C. E., 58
Reckitt, M. B., 14, 33, 43, 46, 58, 154
Ricardo, D., 78
Richards, R. D., 33
Rivière, M. de la, 36
Robbins, L., 86, 107
Roberts, M., 107
Robertson, H. M., 17, 33
Roethligsberger, F. J., 140, 156
Röpke, W., 23, 29 f., 33, 96, 107
Rosenstock-Huessy, E., 93, 107
Rousseau, J. J., 60
Ruskin, John, 50
Russell, Bertrand, 191
Ruysbroek, 88

Santayana, G., 190, 197
Saurat, D., 108
Schumpeter, J. A., 30, 34, 94, 107
Schweitzer, A., 165, 176
Shaftesbury, Lord, 139, 156
Shaw, Bernard, 11
Sleigh, R. S., 16, 33
Smith, Adam, 22, 25, 33, 66, 77, 79
Sombart, Werner, 18, 21, 26, 33, 123
Spencer, Herbert, 25, 42, 130, 136, 156
Spengler, O., 139
Sprat, T., 77
Stalin, Joseph, 90
Stark, W., 34, 58

Steele, R., 43
Sturzo, L., 107

Tawney, R. H., 11, 14, 16, 17, 21, 24, 30, 33, 34, 39, 43, 58, 80
Thurnwald, R. C., 84
Tillich, P., 169 f., 176
de Tocqueville, 60, 107
Toynbee, A., 158, 192, 197
Trevelyan, G. M., 58
Troeltsch, E., 16
Trotsky, L., 90
Twain, Mark, 144, 156

Wagner, D. O., 58
Webb, Sidney and Beatrice, 11, 159
Weber, Max, 16, 17, 18, 26, 33, 44, 81, 107
Westcott, Bishop B. F., 54
Whately, Archbishop, 43, 58
Whitehead, T. N., 34
Whitehead, A. N., 57, 71, 76
Whitman, W., 125
Whyte, L. L., 123 f.
Wilberforce, W., 51, 58
Wilde, O., 154
Willey, B., 156
Wilson, A. R., 84
Wilson, Woodrow, 97
Wissel, Clark, 82, 85
Wolsey, Cardinal, 82

Index of Subjects

Absolute, The, 70
Activism, 182
Adam, The Second, 181
Africa, 32, 53
African Bishops, 53
Agnosticism, 125
Agriculture, 52
Aims, 62 ff.
Altruism, 110, 147, 153
Anomie, 169, 176
Anxiety, 84
Aristocracy, 54

Asceticism, 48, 136
Asia, 32, 99
Associations, 152
Association, Social, 140
Assyrians, 178
Atheism, 125 f.
Australia, 29
Autonomy, 39, 47, 194
Axioms, 62 ff.

Behaviour, Human, 149
Bible, The, 111, 162

Index

Bolshevism, 105
Bourgeois Culture, 31, 56
  Society, 33, 50, 99
  Habits, 156
British labour, 54
Brotherhood, 152

'Cake of Custom', 161
Calling, The, 17 ff., 132 f.
Calvinism, 43, 44, 117, 136
Capitalism, 12, 24, 27, 33, 35, 37, 38, 42, 44, 48, 49, 51, 52, 56, 70, 79 f., 83, 90 ff., 98, 116, 124, 134 ff., 142, 158 ff., 169, 179, 188 f., 193
Capitalism, Rise of, 16
  Decline of, 20, 30, 70
  Definition of, 20 ff.
  Three aspects of, 21 ff.
Charity, 141
China, 171
Christendom, 32, 98, 181 f.
Christian Church, 37, 57, 98, 111
  Culture, 32
  Doctrine, 80
  Social movement, 54
  Thought, 87
Christianity, 60, 86, 119, 168, 188, 192
Church, The, 38, 39, 41
  Church of England, The, 43, 52
Civilization, 26, 147 f., 157 ff., 187
  Frailty of, 153
Civitas, 162
Clan, 101 f.
Classical Economists, 24
Collectivism, 195
Commercial Spirit, 81
Communal Ownership, 141
Communism, 100, 112, 124
Communist Manifesto, 25, 33, 45, 53, 58
Community Consciousness, 140
  Principle, 138
  Sense of, 174
Communities, 152
Competition, 77, 125
Concord, 155
Citizenship, 106

Co-operation, 125
Constituent Assembly, The, 160
Contract, 37, 103 f.
Controlled Economy, 50
Cosmic Process, 124
Creation, 107
Creator, 36, 51, 68
Creatureliness, 114
Cross, The, 41
Culture, 50, 72, 146, 152, 184 ff.
  Western, 56
Czechoslovakia, 175

Decline, Forces of, 157 f.
Deism, 60, 110
Democracy, 112, 131, 195
  Liberal, 135 f.
Determinism, 114
Devil, The, 132
Disintegration, Social, 154
Dissociation, 123, 128 ff., 132
Division of Powers, 41, 98, 181
Division of labour, 171
Duality, 124

Earth, The, 173
East, The, 90
Economic Activity, 185 ff.
  Forces, 49
  Principle, 160
Economics, Classical, 25
Education, 188
Edward VI Schools, 49
Egoism, 152 ff.
Egypt, 98, 107, 165
Elite, 115, 143
Employment, 185 f.
England, 97
English Society, 52
Enlightenment, The, 48, 57, 63, 160
Enterprise, 47
  Free, 139
Equality, 67, 84
Ethics, 87, 103, 142, 161
  Christian, 48, 145
Europe, 26, 90, 130
  Medieval, 81

Index

European Culture, 83
   Dynasties, 97
   Man, 69
   Society, 37, 75, 158
   Tradition, 71, 79, 136
Evangelicalism, 52
Evil, 152
Evolution, 125, 128
Exchange, Laws of, 25

Fabians, 92
Factory Act, 52, 53
   System, 23
Fall of Man, The, 107, 141 f.
Fallenness of Man, 86
Fascism, 112
Faust, 123
Formal Mind, 171 ff.
Free Market, 138, 141
French Revolution, 99, 107
Function, 95 f.
Future Life, 118

German Spirit, 120
Germanic Religion, 105
Germany, 90, 99
God, 36, 87, 116, 122, 132, 141, 146, 152, 161, 174 f., 177 ff., 192, 196
   Will of, 177 ff.
   Spirit of, 191
Good and Evil, 65
Gospel, The, 168
Government, 94, 103, 151
Greece, 82
Greek Rationality, 57, 67
Growth, Forces of, 157 f.
Guild Socialists, 54

Hegelianism, 13
Hebrews, The, 107
   Epistle to, 182
High Church Movement, 53
History, 73, 128, 162
   Meaning of, 181 ff.
Holiness, 141
Holy Grail, 31
Human Nature, 37, 134 ff.

Humanism, 57
Humanists, 124
Humanity, Religion of, 126

Idealism, 89
   Moral, 115
Image of God, 88, 161
Imagination, 73
Independence, Economic, 38
Individualism, 195
Individuality, 152
Industrial Civilization, 140, 154
   Development, 147
   Revolution, 23, 117
   Society, 28
Industrialism, 46, 51, 93 f., 101
Insatiability, 174 f.
Interests, Self-, 140, 142 ff.
   Community of, 109
   Harmony of, 37, 136
   Identity of, 77
   Common, 152
Italy, 99

Jacobinism, 140 f.
Jesuits, 17
Jesus Christ, 69, 145
John, St., Gospel of, 123
Justitia, 80 f.

Kingdom of God, 115, 139, 150, 162
   of Heaven, 47, 149 f., 168
Kingship, 97
Knowledge, 148

Laissez-faire, 22, 27, 35, 37, 45, 78, 80, 109, 135
Language, 84
Law, 66, 103, 133
Layers, Social, 50, 89
Lex Naturae, 37, 74
Liberal Age, 59, 67, 79
   Culture, 27, 71
   Era, 59, 61, 67
   Doctrine, 68
   Idea, 71
Liberalism, 37, 44, 64 f., 69, 71, 84

Index

Liberty, 63 ff.
Love, 149
Lucifer, 88

Machine, Law of the, 171
Man, Nature of, 87
Manchester School, 21
Market, Self-regulating, 80
   Economy, 22 ff., 29 ff., 37, 46, 55, 56, 90, 92, 94, 138
   Principle, 102
Marxism, 27, 112, 117
Materialism, 47, 89, 112
Medieval World, 15
Mercantilism, 77
Mesopotamia, 98, 107
Methodism, 43, 52
Middle Ages, 32
Modern Mind, 116
Modern Thought, 37
Monarchy, 54
Motives, Human, 140 ff.

National Socialism, 120
   Socialists, 46
Nationalism, 112
Natura, 138 f., 161
Natural Law, 66
   Order, 187, 197
   Rights, 66
Nature, 47, 51, 61, 73 f., 79, 81, 88, 103, 112, 114, 118, 121 f., 124 f., 127 ff., 133, 161 ff., 169, 181, 196
Nature, Law of, 84
Nazi Revolution, 90
New England, 29
New Testament, 166, 178, 181
Nineteenth Century, 27, 129
Nonconformist Conscience, 43
North America, 149

Omnipotence, 178
Organism, 42
Ownership, 46
Oxford Movement, 14

Paganism, 111
Papal Encyclicals, 43

Paradise, 86 f., 89
Peace, 155
Physiocrats, 36, 44
Pietism, 110
Piety, 190 f.
Planning, 28
Pleonexia, 189
Politics, 39, 152, 184 ff.
Poor Relief, 27
Pre-capitalist Orders, 93
Predestination, 118
Pre-established Harmony, 36
Profit-motive, 159
Proletarianism, 54, 96
Protection, 78
Protectionism, 92
Providence, 36, 75
Psalm, 119th, 145
Psalmist, 196
Puritanism, 136

Quality Strike, 95

Radicalism, Philosophic, 59 f.
   Liberal, 63
Radicals, 124, 134, 136
Rationalism, 89, 114, 193
Rationality, 169
Reason, 57
Redemption, 139
Reformation, 18, 83
Religion, 35 ff., 41, 57, 87
Religious Consciousness, 56
Renaissance, 75, 83
Revolution, 99
Rituals, 62
Roman Catholics, 43
Romans, The, 165
Romantics, 129
Russia, 171

Sacred Realm, 104
Salvation, 72
Sanctity, 152
Science, 125
Secular, The, 181
Secular Spheres, 47, 87

203

Index

Secularism, 111, 113 ff.
Sin, Original, 136
Sinful World, 151
Sinfulness, 118 f., 141
Socialism, 50, 54, 55, 57, 123, 125, 131, 134 ff., 141, 158 ff., 169
Socialist Society, 37
Society, 42
  Adaptive, 29
  Agrarian, 80 ff., 103
  Civic, 80 ff., 103
  Established, 29
  Sick, 157
Social Sciences, 41
Sociology, 42
South America, 131
Sovereignty, 170
Speenhamland, 27
Spirit, 42, 127 ff., 133, 161 ff., 169
  Centrality of, 183
Spirituality, 114, 190 f.
State, 38, 55, 90 ff., 95, 97, 100, 160
  Fascist, 105
  Liberal, 104
  'Moral', 104
  National, 98
  Omnicompetent, 57, 104
  Secularized, 98
State Collectivism, 51
  Philosophy, 53
  Principle, 55, 90 ff., 94, 101 ff., 160
  Socialism, 55, 95
Statesmanship, 151
Status, 95 f., 104, 154, 169

Technical Civilization, 172
  Reason, 170
  Warfare, 172
Technics, 150, 167
Technology, 140
Theology, 36
Totalitarianism, 41
Trade, 45
Trader Spirit, 123
Trades Unions, 92
Tribal Culture, 26
  Society, 83
Twentieth Century, 27, 40, 53, 97

Universalism, 67
Unwilled Forces, 164
U.S.S.R., 97, 99
Utilitarianism, 109
Utopia, 119

Victorians, 128 ff.
Vitalism, 89, 112
Volk, 46, 105

Wage Labour, 54
Wage, Living, 125
Wesleyan Movement, 72
West, The, 90
Western Civilization, 163, 182
  Culture, 69, 158, 180, 194
  Man, 63, 76, 127, 131, 182
  Mind, 109
  Society, 159, 163 f., 189
  Tradition, 90
  Will, 73